# DOING
# D.A.D.S.

# DOING D.A.D.S.

## INTAKE AND SUPPORT MANUAL

Jeanett and Marvin Charles

*Doing D.A.D.S.: Intake and Support Manual*
First Edition Trade Book, 2022
Copyright © 2022 by Jeanett and Marvin Charles

All rights reserved. No part of this publication may be reproduced, stored in a retrieval system, or transmitted in any form by any means—electronic, mechanical, photocopy, recording, or otherwise—except for brief quotations in critical reviews or articles, without the prior permission of the publisher, except as provided by U.S. copyright law.

To order additional books:
www.aboutdads.org

Visit the D.A.D.S. website at www.aboutdads.org

Published by Anyman Publishing

ISBN: 978-1-952943-12-6

Editorial and Book Packaging: Inspira Literary Solutions, Gig Harbor, WA
Cover Design: mtwDesign, Dickson, TN
Typesetting: PerfecType, Nashville, TN
Printed in the USA by IngramSpark

# Table of Contents

Foreword . . . . . . . . . . . . . . . . . . . . . . . . . . . . . . . . . . . . . . . . . . . . . . . . . . . . . . . . . . . . . . . . . . vii
How to Use This Manual . . . . . . . . . . . . . . . . . . . . . . . . . . . . . . . . . . . . . . . . . . . . . . . . . . ix

## CHAPTER 1

### 1.1 | Who Is D.A.D.S.? . . . . . . . . . . . . . . . . . . . . . . . . . . . . . . . . . . . . . . . . . . . . . . . 3
1.1.a Mission Statement . . . . . . . . . . . . . . . . . . . . . . . . . . . . . . . . . . . . . . . . . . . . . . . . 6
1.1.b Vision . . . . . . . . . . . . . . . . . . . . . . . . . . . . . . . . . . . . . . . . . . . . . . . . . . . . . . . . . . . . 6
1.1.c Disclosure . . . . . . . . . . . . . . . . . . . . . . . . . . . . . . . . . . . . . . . . . . . . . . . . . . . . . . . . 6
1.1.d The Declaration of Fatherhood . . . . . . . . . . . . . . . . . . . . . . . . . . . . . . . . . . . . 6
1.1.e The "Becoming a Better Dad Pledge" . . . . . . . . . . . . . . . . . . . . . . . . . . . . . . 7

### 1.2 | Building Your D.A.D.S. Team . . . . . . . . . . . . . . . . . . . . . . . . . . . . . . . . . . 8
1.2.a Characteristics of the D.A.D.S. Workforce . . . . . . . . . . . . . . . . . . . . . . . . . . 8
1.2.b D.A.D.S. Fundamental Organizational Chart . . . . . . . . . . . . . . . . . . . . . . 12

### 1.3 | Intake and Engagement Process: Setting SMART Goals . . . 14
1.3.a Preparing for the Intake Interview . . . . . . . . . . . . . . . . . . . . . . . . . . . . . . . . 15

### 1.4 | Welcome to D.A.D.S. . . . . . . . . . . . . . . . . . . . . . . . . . . . . . . . . . . . . . . . . . . 17
1.4.a Examples of Intake Forms . . . . . . . . . . . . . . . . . . . . . . . . . . . . . . . . . . . . . . . 20

### 1.5 | Terms and Abbreviations . . . . . . . . . . . . . . . . . . . . . . . . . . . . . . . . . . 25
1.5.a Preparing for Incoming Call/Interview . . . . . . . . . . . . . . . . . . . . . . . . . . . 29
1.5.b Follow Through after Sending Intake Forms . . . . . . . . . . . . . . . . . . . . . . 30

## CHAPTER 2

### 2.1 | Child Support Assistance . . . . . . . . . . . . . . . . . . . . . . . . . . . . . . . . . . . 33

## 2.2 | Administrative vs Court-Ordered ..... 36
2.2.a Modifications ..... 36
    Arrears ..... 38

# CHAPTER 3

## 3.1 | Parenting Plan Assistance ..... 41

## 3.2 | Establishing Parentage ..... 47

## 3.3 | Developing a Parenting Plan ..... 50
3.3.a Temporary ..... 50
3.3.b Modification ..... 51
3.3.c Case Schedule ..... 51
3.3.d Example of a Completed Parenting Plan ..... 51

# CHAPTER 4

## 4.1 | Scheduling Appointments ..... 135

## 4.2 | Scanning Documents ..... 137

## 4.3 | Telephone Guide ..... 138

## 4.4 | Training Instructions for ILINX ..... 139

# CHAPTER 5

## 5.1 | Ongoing Client Support ..... 147

## 5.2 | Support Meetings ..... 149

## 5.3 | Fatherhood Training ..... 151

Acknowledgments ..... 159
About the Authors ..... 160

# Foreword by Marvin Charles

It has been said that I am the face of D.A.D.S. I like to say that my wife, Jeanett, is the brain. Jeanett has reached about 250 new clients PER YEAR, most of them formerly incarcerated men who learn about the program from other fathers or probation officers.

In the beginning, almost all were African American. Now, our client base includes Whites, Blacks, Muslims, Christians, Hispanic, Asians. If you were to ask my wife and me, that would be one of the things about D.A.D.S. we'd say we are most proud of. In the words of my wife, "No matter who they are or where they come from, most men are seeking help with child support payments, and they want to develop parenting plans to help establish visitation or gain custody of their children." In helping them accomplish these goals, Jeanett doesn't do the work for them, but rather uses what she knows to help them navigate the system and become their own advocates. She helps them understand the language of the system, which often requires them to unlearn the language of the streets.

In telling the story of D.A.D.S., I like to share Jeanett's and my own story. Overwhelmed by drug use, Jeanett (who was my girlfriend at the time) and I were incapable of caring for our newborn daughter. So, in 1998, when the baby was only months old, I took her down to a local hospital, intending to leave her there on the steps of the hospital.

But I couldn't bring myself to abandon my child, and instead I took her to a women's shelter, which directed me to Child Protective Services. The state at the time had custody of four of my other children and had been searching for both Jeanett and me.

Jeanett and I had been in and out of rehab, struggling to remain clean. I realized I was doing to my children what had been done to me. I too had been raised in the foster care system. I knew I had to stay in this fight. And, when a CPS worker suggested marriage to prevent termination of our parental rights, I asked Jeanett to marry me. That year, we entered into an improbable marriage that launched us on a long, difficult path to rebuild not just our own troubled lives, but to bring together our seven children.

When the state began garnishing our paychecks to cover back child support, Jeanett began working to modify the withdrawals to relieve the burden on the family. It took us three years to get all our children back, earning us the Atlantic Street Center's Family of the Year Award in Seattle.

Because of all the knowledge Jeanett gleaned while working with DCS, she came to understand the diverse and complicated laws around child support and parenting. It was then that we started wondering if we could take what she and I had learned to help those people we'd previously gotten high with, done crime with, and done time with.

It is our prayer and vision that this *Doing DADS Intake and Support Manual* will become a valued resource of the immediate future for potential nonprofit organizations and individuals with the heart for dads who desire to be reconnected with their child(ren). We hope it will provide the necessary insights for those who feel the call to become "System Navigators"—community caregivers and support personnel who will help reduce the negative impact of father absence on families and restore hope and joy to fathers and children everywhere.

*Marvin Charles*
*Founder and Director*
*Divine Alternatives for Dads Services*

# How to Use This Manual

If you have picked up this manual, it's because someone you know is disconnected from their children, and desperately wants to regain a place in their lives.

You want to help.

And that's what D.A.D.S. is all about, plain and simple: a helping community of caring friends working together to reunite families.

To start your own D.A.D.S. program, you will need:

- a starting team of two to three volunteers, willing to work in community, with shared values and beliefs and a heart for seeing people restored to God's design for their lives
- these two to three people to have testimonies of their own of how they overcame similar circumstances of being alienated from their families due to addictions, incarceration, legal problems, homelessness, or other issues (this is important)
- a willingness to share your own story and to listen, support, and walk with people through their journeys of overcoming
- availability to help clients navigate the legal, technical, emotional, relational, and spiritual obstacles along the way to family reunification

Of course, you can add to this core group as needs arise (especially administratively), but this is the foundation of your team.

Basically, what D.A.D.S. is about, at the community level, is caring. It's walking with people who have never felt heard, never been respected, and have never been extended a helping hand of dignity and friendship to start the path back to wholeness for themselves and their families.

More often than not, they will come in, the first time they see you, filled with the guilt and shame of their current situation, and the hopelessness of not feeling understood in it.

Marvin and I were both once in this situation, and we have never forgotten it. It was why we started D.A.D.S., and why we still serve our community today. What has made D.A.D.S. the pillar of success it is today is the chorus of past clients saying things like, "For the first time, someone heard my voice, listened to my story, and was willing to stand with me."

And that, in a nutshell, is how we "do D.A.D.S." Everything in this manual, every instruction, every procedure, every form that needs to be filled out, has this at its core.

Your job, as a D.A.D.S representative, is first to listen. After that, it's to help your client navigate whatever his particular case requires to fulfill obligations of the state and re-establish a relationship with his children, and possibly the mother(s) of his children.

Secondarily, your job is to provide a support system, a family, to re-establish your client's confidence in himself and in the greater community. Many of your clients will have experienced this in childhood, whether through their nuclear or extended family, church, or other support systems from which they have become disconnected. Many times, their experience with you will trigger these strong memories of their parents, their faith, and other important relationships. Your caring investment in their lives will lay down the foundation for these important parts of their lives to be restored.

D.A.D.S. certainly doesn't have the corner on this market, but we have learned something remarkable in our 20-plus years of ministry: the most important thing people need to get on the road to restoration is CARING.

All the rest is just paperwork.

*Jeanett Charles*

# CHAPTER ONE

# :: DATA AT D.A.D.S ::
## DIVINE ALTERNATIVES FOR DADS SERVICES

**Since 2019, when DADS started collecting data in a new way, the following outcomes were reported.**\*

- **109** fathers reported reunification with their children.
- **116** fathers reported having attended a parenting class.
- **105** fathers reported having obtained housing/employment.
- **33** fathers reported having improved the relationship with their child or the other parent.
- **21** fathers reported completing substance abuse treatment

\*All outcomes are voluntarily self-reported by clients.

**Since 1998, DADS has served**

**4,728** fathers / parents

**12,573** babies / children

**So far in 2021, DADS has served**

**379** fathers / parents

**678** babies / children

### Most Utilized Services at DADS
- Child Support
- Custody and Visitation
- Parenting Plans
- Spiritual Guidance
- Re-Entry Support

### Why DADS?
"[They] gave me confidence that I am on the right track [and that] there is hope."

### So far in 2021...
**82%** of fathers identify as men of color

**48%** of fathers report a history of incarceration

October 2021

Prepared by: The Capacity Collective

## 1.1 Who Is D.A.D.S.?

D.A.D.S. is a grassroots organization 501(c)(3), located in Washington State, that is leading a movement to turn the tide on the epidemic of father absence in America. D.A.D.S. gives hope to fathers seeking re-unification with their children by walking together in supportive community and helping navigate relational and legal barriers which separate them from their children and families.

D.A.D.S.' services include:

- Family Reunification
- Case Management
- Child Support Management
- Parenting Plan Assistance
- Parenting Classes
- Support Groups
- Assistance Securing/Filling out Court and Other Documents
- Other Resources

## Beginnings

**Marvin and Jeanett Charles** are the co-founders of D.A.D.S. Their own personal story is one of overcoming and transformation, and an ongoing legacy of bringing similar transformation to their own community, and to other communities around the country through the work of D.A.D.S.

Marvin Charles' mother, Doris Brooks, was a 14-year-old ninth-grader in Seattle when he was born. One day, unexpectedly, Doris's mother gave six-month-old Marvin up for adoption while Doris was at school. Although Marvin grew up in a home not far from the Brooks' home, the two did not meet again until four decades later, when she contacted adoption consultant Karen King, who quickly found Marvin. Their dramatic reunification story made national headlines.

By that time, Marvin and Jeanett Charles had already lost three children to the state's foster care system, and Marvin was on the verge of leaving their newborn daughter on the steps of a hospital because he and Jeanett were both deep in drug addiction. But he couldn't walk away. "I couldn't do to my child what had been done to me," said Marvin, who had painful experiences in the foster care system after the death of his adoptive mother.

When, in 1997, CPS (Child Protective Services) informed Marvin and Jeanett that they could permanently lose custody of their children, this triggered powerful change in their lives. With help from God, Marvin and Jeanett had the courage and determination to move beyond their history of drugs and alcohol, interventions by Child Protective Services, unlawful behavior, homelessness, and promiscuity.

Marvin and Jeanett decided to marry, get sober, and become committed to reuniting their family. They worked hard, got jobs, and learned how to deal with dependency court and caseworkers. In three years, their children were returned to them, and they'd earned the Atlantic Street Center's Family of the Year Award.

In the process of rebuilding their lives, Marvin and Jeanett learned to be voices for their community. They also recognized how the challenges of raising children and becoming new homeowners required new skills in managing family change and development.

"We started asking, 'How can we use what we've learned the hard way to help other people who had been through what we'd been through?' " Marvin said. "How could we help reduce the destructive results of fatherlessness in low-income communities of color?" The couple launched D.A.D.S. in 1999 out of their living room with the help of a $15,000 grant.

In 2004, D.A.D.S. opened a storefront office in Seattle, Washington. Many volunteers and generous donors have helped make this office a family-centered house of healing and redemption. Men who receive D.A.D.S. services learn how to overcome child support debt, build financial and personal stability, and reunite in positive relationships with their children and families.

As their problems begin to resolve, some of these men desire to marry and create a stable home for their children. It is an added reward when a man discovers the grace of God, and begins to experience healthy relationships for the first time in his life.

In the 20-plus years since D.A.D.S. was founded, Marvin and Jeanett and their staff have helped more than 4,700 fathers. All D.A.D.S. services are free, so that income is never a barrier to their clients. Marvin and Jeanett are regularly invited to speak at local, state, and national fatherhood and family conferences and events. They have built strong relationships with leadership at Washington State's Division of Child Support and Department of Social and Health Services, which allows them to work cooperatively to help D.A.D.S. clients, and advocate for policies that make a positive difference for the families they serve.

Seven of the Charles' eight children are now grown and in college or working, and one is still at home as of the time of this writing. Their family and community leadership are living testimony of hope to the fathers that come to them.

### 1.1.a  D.A.D.S. Mission Statement

To give fathers hope by walking in supportive community, helping fathers navigate relational and legal barriers which separate them from their children and families.

### 1.1.b  Vision

Stronger fathers leading to healthier and vibrant communities.

### 1.1.c  Disclosure Statement

From the beginning of our interactions with prospective clients, we want to give full disclosure of what we have to offer them (and what we don't). By "disclosure," we mean **communicating the nature of our services immediately** when clients make an initial contact with D.A.D.S. When working at the front desk with fathers/mothers, it is important to remember, and to make it clear, that we are not lawyers and we are not able to represent our clients. We do not ask for payment. We cannot guarantee the outcomes, but we are willing to help by finding an open door to walk through. We can give suggestions based on our knowledge and experience; however, we do not give advice. The fathers/mothers will fill out their forms, file them in court, and go to court hearings on their own. The fathers/mothers make the final choice as to what terms they request on the forms. Our role is to be their support team and help them complete whatever tasks or action steps are being asked of them in their reunification process.

### 1.1.d  The Declaration of Fatherhood

The Declaration of Fatherhood is a statement of intention that we share with fathers, and encourage them to make it their own. We suggest printing this out, framing it, and hanging it in a prominent place in the office where you will be receiving D.A.D.S. clients:

> *I am a man; I am a father. My heart is for my children, and my community.*
> *I have witnessed the destruction of father absence.*
> *I know I have the power to do something about it. So, today, I say, "Enough!"*
> *Today, I will work to quench my father thirst.*
> *Tomorrow, I will work to quench my community's father thirst.*
> *Because I am a man called to be a father, I am a man and father with the power to quench the father thirst.*

## 1.1.e  The Becoming a Better Dad Pledge

Similarly, we encourage you to share the following pledge with your clients, and display it in a prominent place where you will be receiving them:

*To become a better dad,*
*I will turn my life around,*
*face the truth, and break free from the things*
*that at one time held me down.*

*To become a better dad,*
*I will commit to being there*
*for the sake of my child*
*by investing this time here.*

*To become a better dad,*
*I will do what men do:*
*mature, respect women, and love and serve others.*
*That includes my children too.*

*To become a better dad,*
*I need healing from my past—*
*all the hurt, trauma, and failures—*
*forgiving, making amends, moving forward at last.*

*To become a better dad,*
*I will be humble and seek to learn*
*ways to improve as a parent, co-parent, and citizen,*
*and let this passion to be better burn within me.*

*I will become a better dad;*
*no matter how tough it is, I will not quit or give up,*
*through the support of my faith, family, and community,*
*until my last breath and my eyes finally shut.*

## 1.2 Building Your Team

### D.A.D.S. Core Service Delivery:

- Intake
- Assessment of Service Needs
- Child Support Management
- Parenting Plan Assistance
- Child Family Unification
- Parenting Classes
- Assistance Securing/Filling out Court and Other Documents
- Fathering Support Groups
- D.A.D.S. Fathering Case Management

### 1.2a Characteristics of the D.A.D.S. Workforce

As we think about replicating the D.A.D.S. service delivery model, it is important to note that success is based on carefully conducting the service areas mentioned above. Of these services areas, it is the last two—Fathering Support Groups and D.A.D.S. Fathering Case Management—that provide the greatest opportunity for D.A.D.S. staff to establish the long-term connections with fathers that contribute to their long-term success.

There are a number of issues to consider related to the D.A.D.S. work force, especially those that arise when working directly with the fathers. As you will certainly agree, it is the long-term relationships and associations with fathers that will foster lasting success for them engaging or re-engaging with their children.

Most community-based, social-betterment programs have a primary purpose of enhancing the livability of their clients and/or community members. The most important assets of these organizations are the frontline staff members who are doing the work. It is therefore necessary to provide some context to any organization that is considering replicating the D.A.D.S. model. There are some characteristics and expectations of the D.A.D.S. frontline staff that are non-negotiable and must be adhered to when building a D.A.D.S. workforce.

## Connecting with Fathers

We believe that D.A.D.S. services start with developing a genuine, individualized connection between the fathers and D.A.D.S. staff. The connection is always based on the trust, experience, and consistency that fathers perceive from the D.A.D.S. staff. Furthermore, a contributing factor to the effectiveness of D.A.D.S. services is the empathy and compassion demonstrated by D.A.D.S. staff to the fathers.

We further believe that the self-disclosure of the staff member's prior life experience, related to poor or absentee fathering, presents a connecting opportunity for fathers.

As the fathers perceive the D.A.D.S. staff as having walked a mile in their shoes, a father usually adopts a sense of trust and loyalty, thereby becoming far more willing to share his actual situation more openly, honestly, and consistently. We therefore believe it is vital for each D.A.D.S. staff to become capable of sharing their own "fathering story." It is usually through hearing portions of the staff member's personal story that a connection is made with the father, compelling him to find hope and belief in the possibility of change in his own life.

**Empathy:** *refers to the ability to relate to another's pain vicariously, as if one has experienced that pain themselves.*

**Compassion:** *refers to sympathy and concern for the suffering of others and the desire to alleviate such suffering.*

As fathers participate in D.A.D.S. support groups, as well as being individually case managed, the long-term connections to D.A.D.S. is initiated and fostered. D.A.D.S. makes no distinction between the father who is in need of assistance with completing a simple legal form versus a father needing assistance and support with navigating a complex situation related to his child. D.A.D.S. tries to develop a lasting connection and relationship with ALL fathers who show up. We find community value in personally being available for every father who is referred or walks through the door.

## Value Added through Lived Life Experience

Consistent with national data related to workforces that provide "lived life experience," D.A.D.S. finds value in our frontline staff (those working directly with fathers) having had the prior lived experience of working through the D.A.D.S. program themselves, to become engaged or reengaged with their own children, and thereby having their own fathering story of struggle and triumph to share with fathers.

It is important that D.A.D.S. staff model healthy fathering relationships as a means of creating healthier fathers and families. We don't want to just teach this; we want to be this. At D.A.D.S., we believe that we must be the change that we wish to see in the world.

> *Organizations that incorporate community members with lived life experience are better equipped to make their services more focused, efficient, and integrated.*

## D.A.D.S. Core Motivation

At D.A.D.S., we believe that faith in GOD is the most powerful and real agent for redemptive change that there is. **While we serve all, regardless of their faith,** we put our complete trust in what GOD has called us to do. His Word says that He will supply what we need as sons and daughters of God.

> *We further believe that GOD, even more than us, yearns to reunite children and parents. When we do not have the answers, GOD does. It is not all up to us or up to any of our clients. We act on what we understand, and trust in GOD for what we do not.*

## Value Added Through the Team Approach to Service Delivery:

## The D.A.D.S. Workforce Team

At D.A.D.S., we believe in, and value, the process of working as a team. We therefore advocate and provide staff training activities aimed at team building. As part of the team-building process, it becomes necessary that all team members understand their roles and responsibilities as well as those of other team members. Even though the frontline Intake Specialists are charged with directly working with the fathers, all staff understand and/or are capable of administering the D.A.D.S. core curriculum.

It is a priority of D.A.D.S. administrators and program coordinators to work closely with D.A.D.S. frontline staff, encouraging team participation with every father, when possible. The D.A.D.S. staff are encouraged to mirror the change they advocate to fathers. It is a goal of the D.A.D.S. organization to support and empower all staff to become experts at providing the D.A.D.S. service delivery model, as well as strive for professionalism in working with the many stakeholder agencies that D.A.D.S. works with.

Vital to the D.A.D.S. team approach, all staff must:

- know and understand the D.A.D.S. organizational mission, goals, and vision for the future
- understand their particular roles and responsibilities as well as the roles and responsibilities of other team members
- help to develop and maintain an organizational culture of team problem solving
- respect and participate in an environment of client confidentiality
- help to promote an organizational environment that is client centered
- help to promote an organizational environment that functions through clear and concise communication processes
- model healthy fathering relationships as a means of creating healthier fathers and families
- help facilitate the dismantling of shame by inviting fathers to discuss their stories in the presence of others sharing the same experience
- contribute to a trauma-informed service environment

## D.A.D.S. Community Building

We believe that stakeholder outreach becomes central to the growth and development of the D.A.D.S. organization. Designated staff must become capable of providing presentations to a wide range of community stakeholders. The D.A.D.S. presentations MUST be consistent among the D.A.D.S. staff. We never want to disseminate conflicting information regarding D.A.D.S. services.

Because of the environmental differences and uniqueness of the different communities, each specific D.A.D.S. site will determine the necessary stakeholders and community partners. Though some stakeholders such as DHS and Child Support offices are necessary to every D.A.D.S. site, there may also be those stakeholders that might be unique, yet important to a particular community.

## 1.2b D.A.D.S. FUNDAMENTAL ORGANIZATIONAL CHART

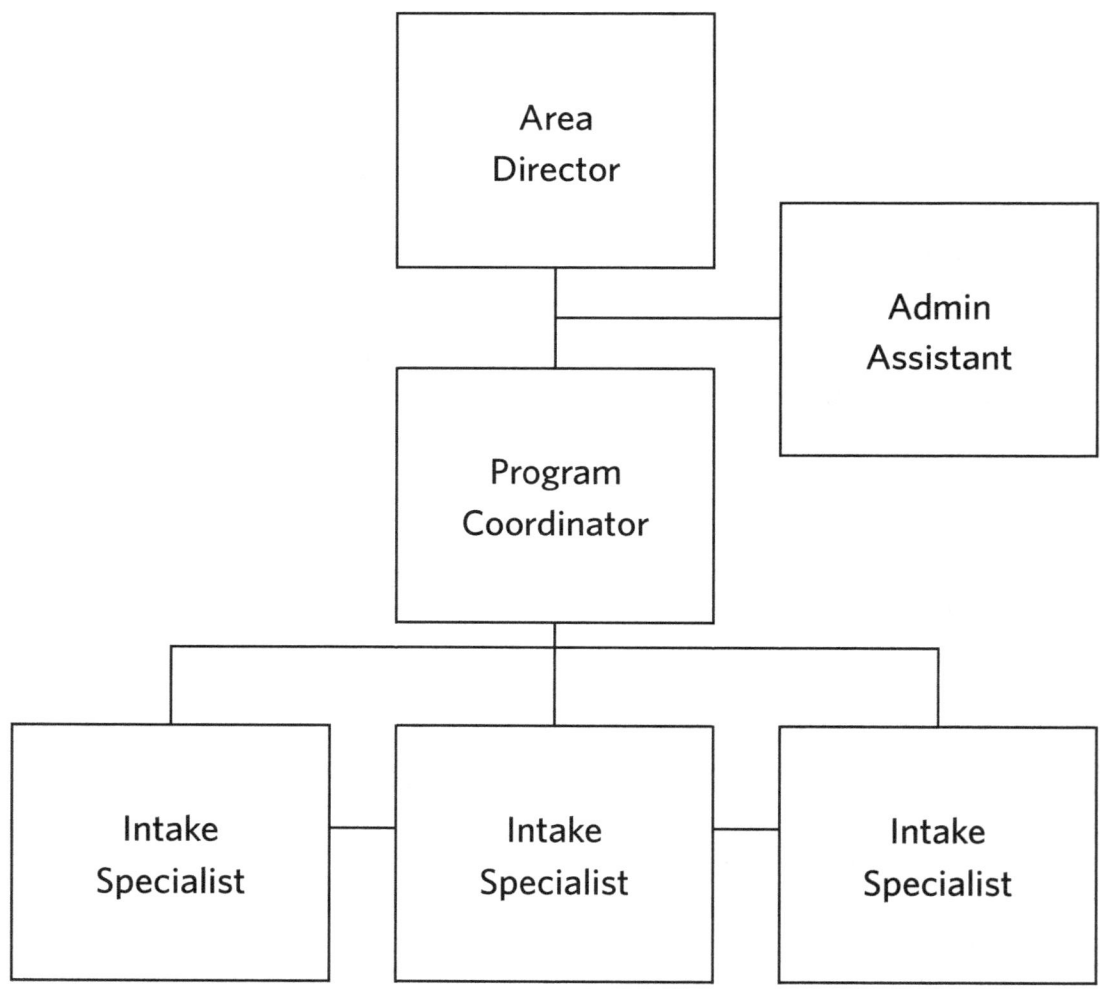

**AREA DIRECTOR:** Administrative responsibilities include but are not limited to: budget development, budget management, public relations, staff management, organizational planning, contract procurement, contract compliance, contract reporting, fundraising, reporting out to the Board of Directors, and other duties as assigned by the Board of Directors.

**PROGRAM COORDINATOR:** Coordinating responsibilities include but are not limited to: staff management, client case review, client resource development, class facilitation, support group facilitation, community relations, program service oversight, and other duties as assigned by the Area Director.

**INTAKE SPECIALIST:** Responsibilities include but are not limited to: client intake, client assessment, case development, group facilitation, family mediation, individual coaching, family coaching, and other duties as assigned by Program Coordinator.

**ADMINSTRATIVE ASSISTANT:** Responsibilities include but are not limited to: clerical support and assistance, program correspondence support, phone/electronic communication support, direct support to the Area Director and Program Coordinator, appointment scheduling, office management, and other duties as assigned by the Area Director.

## 1.3 Intake and Engagement Process / Setting SMART Goals

Before determining if D.A.D.S. can be a resource to a potential client—and how—it is first helpful to spend a bit of time with the person, hearing their story and determining if their situation makes them a good candidate for D.A.D.S. services. Through personal conversation, listen to them, ask good questions, and try to ascertain what their goals are. Try to determine if their objectives are:

1. **Specific: Define the goal as much as possible with no unclear language.**
    a. WHO is involved, WHAT do they want to accomplish, WHERE will it be done, WHY are they doing this (reasons, purpose), and WHICH constraints and/or requirements do they have?
    b. After you have had a chance to sit down and get to know the person during the engagement beginning process, then you can continue onto the intake process. Remember: we are here to work from our hearts and not just push papers at our clients.
2. **Measurable: Is it possible to track the progress and measure the outcome?**
    a. How much, how many, etc.—how will we know when the goal is accomplished?
    b. This is where we build rapport with the client and gain their trust, and assure them that we are here to help them through their journey every step of the way. Not all clients will update us and we may never hear back from some, but we want to offer that open door for them to know that we are available to them.
3. **Attainable/Achievable: Is their goal reasonable enough to be accomplished? How so?**
    a. Make sure the client's goal in not out of reach or below what they are capable of.
    b. We want to support our clients in reconnecting in their children's lives; we have to make sure that they are ready for what they are asking for realistically. We don't want to set them up for failure nor give them false hopes.

4. **Relevant: Is the goal worthwhile and will it meet the child(ren)'s needs?**
    a. Is each goal consistent with other goals the client has established, and does it fit with their immediate and long-term goals?
    b. We want to see families come together for a common goal in reuniting, but there has to be a relevant want. We don't want to see that our help is due to a dispute between parents that has nothing to do with the children. We want to have a concrete purpose in what we are doing. As you engage with a client in Step 1, you will see if they are truly there for the children, or for another reason.

Be sure to allow enough time with a client to be able to discern the above through personal conversation. Your objective should include blocking out appropriate time for clients when setting appointments; we do not want our clients to feel rushed.

   a. This portion will help us in the case management process of setting goals and obtaining them.
   b. This will help you establish where your client is at with their sense of urgency as well as give them some time to think about what they are getting themselves into when it comes to the court processes. Everything takes time and is a process.

If we take our time and follow the engagement process of getting to know our clients on an individual basis first, we can help them to the fullest ability of our D.A.D.S. expectations. The "intake" of the client is part of the process, but do not lose sight of what's important to us first.

Note: This may be your client's first experience of someone actually listening to his story, and feeling respected and heard. It is not uncommon for this to be an emotional experience. Have Kleenex and a willing shoulder if your client wants to have a good cry. This is perfectly okay and will often clear the road for more objective conversations afterward, once that part is out of the way. An arm around the shoulder and an empathetic response will go a long way.

## 1.3a Preparing for the Intake Interview

There are four forms that should already be in the intake folder for each new client before officially beginning to process their case as a D.A.D.S. client (copies of these forms are provided for you at the end of this section). Note that we are providing sample forms from Washington State, our home state, for this manual. If you are in another state, you will need to become familiar with your own state's similar forms.

1. **DSHS Authorization:** When a father/mother signs this form, he/she gives us permission to work with the Division of Child Support (DCS) on his or her behalf and to receive detailed reports and information from DCS related to the case(s).
2. **D.A.D.S. Client Intake Form:** This form gives us important information about the client, his/her children, and specific demographics that may help us as we proceed. For example if a father states he is there for help with visitation and we see that he marked he was just released from incarceration in the last 90 days, we will know what further questions may need to be asked in helping in his case. We will also use the demographics in order to help us in grant reporting, presentation to donors, and government agencies as well as our own internal analysis of who we are reaching in our community through our organization.
3. **Service Episode Record:** This is for our internal use to document why the client came into our office, what the situation is in a brief synopsis. as well as the next steps he/she will need to take in the process.
4. **D.A.D.S. Services Evaluation Form:** This form is used to evaluate the customer service that was received.

# 1.4 Welcome to D.A.D.S.

1. We are going to assume you have some sort of office space or meeting place set up for your D.A.D.S. ministry. When the client walks in, welcome them and make them comfortable (seating, water, etc.).
2. Ask the client to sign a sign-in sheet you have created for this purpose, to create a record of their visit.
3. Ask the client if they have ever been to D.A.D.S. before. Whether yes or no, look them up in both ILINX and Apricot. (If you are using these programs, see Chapter 4 for system instructions. You may elect to use another CMS, Client Management System, of your choosing.)
   a. If the client has been into the office prior, make sure there is an updated intake form with current address and phone number information. If the client is there for child support assistance, have them fill out a new authorization form **only if they do not have one on file already.** These do not expire unless otherwise noted on the paperwork; a previous form will still be valid for use.
   b. If the client has not been to the office before, then take the four forms listed in section 1.2 out of a premade folder, place them onto a clipboard, and hand them to the client with a pen.
      i. DSHS Authorization Form: Ask the client to fill out the boxes with either a red mark or gray shading (depending on how the document was printed) and then print, sign, and date the form.
      ii. D.A.D.S. Client Intake Form: Ask him/her to fill out everything on this sheet with exception of the file location that is for internal office use. Ask the client to list all biological children, not just the one(s) they are here about.
      iii. Service Episode Record: Instruct him/her to only fill out the date, name, and social security fields on this form as you will fill out the SER portion.
      iv. D.A.D.S. Services Evaluation Form: Make sure you remember to collect this form at the end of the interview.

4. Once you have the first three forms completed, you will sign the DSHS Authorization form on the witness/notary line on the bottom right of the page. Next you will write "sent" with today's date and your initials in the top right hand corner of the page. Scan and email the form to DSHS and place it back in the folder.
5. Fill out the Access and Visitation sheet on the front desk clipboard with the information taken directly from the intake form. If the client marked "self" as the referral source, inquire more as to how he/she heard about D.A.D.S.
6. After completing your interview with the client, continue on to input the client's information and demographics into the database; in the meantime, take out their Service Episode Record and be ready to take notes as to why the client is there and what steps D.A.D.S. will provide in assisting them in their journey.

## Scenarios and Where to Begin

1. A father comes into the office and says that he hasn't seen his child(ren) in some time and the mother refuses to let him have anything to do with the child(ren). Clarify the below key points and then refer to Chapter 3 for the possibility of creating a parenting plan to help with the visitation between him and the children.
    a. Verify with the father if he has established legal parentage or if he signed an Acknowledgment of Parentage form at the hospital when the child was born.
    b. Does he have a copy of the birth certificate? If not, we would direct him to the nearest vital statistics office to obtain one as it is required in order to file a parenting plan.
    c. Does he know where the mother lives or works? This is important to know where to serve her documents, as they pertain to the court case if the father elects to go through the process of obtaining a parenting plan.
    d. What is his current situation? He can't be homeless, living in a shelter, or in transitional housing and expect to have his children overnight every other weekend.
    e. Is he prepared for a realistic and feasible schedule with the children? Depending on their ages, they may be in school and have extracurricular activities that might need to be taken in account when setting a schedule.
2. A mother comes in and inquires how she can get help with her child support case as she is paying 50% of her wages, leaving her with the bare minimum to try to survive. She wants to do the right thing but she has no extra money to pay for the supervised visits that are required as part of her parenting plan. Clarify the below key points and then refer to Chapter 2 for child support assistance.

a. Was the child support case started due to a court order or is this case an administrative order through the Division of Child Support (DCS)?
   b. When was the last time that you had a modification or a review hearing?
   c. Have you tried to contact DCS and explain your situation and see if they will work with you?
   d. Were your wages more or less when the child support case was established? Can you bring in one month's worth of paystubs for us to look at in helping you with your child support documentation?
3. A man comes to the front desk and explains that he just saw on some form of social media that his ex-girlfriend recently had a baby and he thinks it is his. He wants to know what to do to establish paternity and to have visitation with his child. Clarify the below key points and then refer to Chapter 3 for establishing parentage.
   a. Does he know if another person signed the Acknowledgement of Parentage?
   b. Was he married to the mother at the time of the child's birth?
4. A father calls and is upset that the current parenting plan isn't being followed. The mother of his children has a new boyfriend/husband, and the new boyfriend/husband feels he has the right to dictate the relationship between the father and the children. Clarify the below key points and then refer to Chapter 3 for the possibility of filing a contempt to the current parenting plan or modifying the existing parenting plan. Ask the client:
   a. Was the parenting plan finalized through court proceedings?
   b. Does the parental agreement section of the parenting plan show the requests that you are making that aren't being followed?
   c. Do you have a copy on hand of the parenting plan so that we can review it with you and provide possible suggestions?
   d. Has this been an ongoing issue or was there a single occurrence between you and the mother in which you might possibly be able to work things out without going back through court?

*sent 01/01/2019*
*Intake specialist to write once sent to DCS*

## Authorization

**AUTHORIZATION TO DISCLOSE DSHS RECORDS OF:**

| NAME LAST | FIRST | MIDDLE | DATE OF BIRTH |
|---|---|---|---|
| DOE | JOHN | ALLEN | 01/01/1977 |

The following information may help in locating records:

**FORMER NAMES**

| CLIENT IDENTIFICATION NUMBER | OTHER IDENTIFICATION NUMBER | DATES OF SERVICE | LOCATION OF SERVICE |
|---|---|---|---|
| 123-45-6789 | | | |

**DISCLOSE TO:**

| NAME LAST | FIRST | MIDDLE | TITLE |
|---|---|---|---|
| | | | |

ORGANIZATION OR BUSINESS NAME IF APPLICABLE

| ADDRESS | CITY | STATE | ZIP CODE |
|---|---|---|---|
| | | | |

| TELEPHONE NUMBER (INCLUDE AREA CODE) | FAX NUMBER (INCLUDE AREA CODE) | E-MAIL ADDRESS |
|---|---|---|
| | | |

REASON FOR DISCLOSURE (NOT REQUIRED)

**AUTHORIZATION:**

SOURCES: I authorize the following DSHS programs to disclose or give access to confidential information about me as described below. Information may be provided verbally or by computer data transfer, mail, fax, or hand delivery.

☐ The following programs only (check all that apply):
- ☐ Behavioral Health and Recovery (DBHR)
- ☐ Child Support (DCS)
- ☐ Developmental Disabilities (DDA)
- ☐ Juvenile Rehabilitation programs
- ☐ Vocational Rehabilitation (DVR)
- ☐ Special Commitment Center (SCC)
- ☐ Children's Administration (CA)
- ☐ Community Services (CSD – public assistance)
- ☐ Home and Community Services (HCS)
- ☐ Residential Care Services (RCS)
- ☐ State Mental Health Institutions (ESH, WSH, CSTC)
- ☐ Human Resources Division
- ☐ Other: _____

☐ All parts of the Department of Social and Health Services (DSHS)

RECORDS: I authorize the following DSHS records to be disclosed:
- ☐ Client records held by parts of DSHS marked above
- ☐ Other confidential records held by parts of DSHS marked above
- ☐ Personal information in employment-related records
- ☐ All my client records
- ☐ Records on the attached list
- ☐ The following records only:

I want to limit the records to be disclosed as follows (by date, type of record, etc.):

PLEASE NOTE: If your client or other confidential records include any of the following information, you must also complete the below section to allow disclosure of these records.

SPECIAL RECORDS: I give my permission to disclose the following information held in DSHS records (check all that apply):
- ☐ HIV/AIDS and STD test results, diagnosis or treatment records (RCW 70.02.220)
- ☐ Mental health records (RCW 70.02.230 or 240)
- ☐ Chemical Dependency (CD) records (42 CFR Part 2)

- This permission is valid for 180 days or ☐ until _____ (date or event, if not checked, will be 180 days).
- I may revoke or withdraw my permission in writing at any time, but that will not affect information already produced.
- I understand that my records may no longer be protected under the laws that apply to DSHS after this they are produced.
- A copy of this form is valid to give my permission to disclose records. DSHS may charge to provide copies of its records.

| AUTHORIZED BY (SIGNATURE) | DATE SIGNED | TELEPHONE NUMBER (INCLUDE AREA CODE) |
|---|---|---|
| *John Allen Doe* | 01/01/2019 | (123) 456-7890 |
| PRINT NAME | WITNESS/NOTARY (SIGN AND PRINT NAME, IF APPLICABLE) | |
| JOHN ALLEN DOE | DADS Intake Specialist to sign here | |

If I am not the person who is the subject of the records, I am authorized to sign because I am the: (attach proof of authority)
☐ Parent of minor  ☐ Legal Guardian  ☐ Personal Representative  ☐ Other:

**Notice to those receiving information:** If these records contain information about HIV, STDs, or alcohol or drug abuse, you may not further disclose that information under federal and state law without specific permission of the subject and meeting specific legal requirements.

AUTHORIZATION
DSHS 17-063 (REV. 02/2016)

## WELCOME TO D.A.D.S. 21

**INSTRUCTIONS FOR COMPLETION OF AUTHORIZATION FORM**

**Purpose:** You should use this form when you want DSHS to be able to disclose confidential information about you to another person (including an attorney, a legislator, or a relative). You may give permission to disclose all confidential records DSHS has about you or you may limit your permission to specific records or parts of the agency. This form will also permit DSHS to discuss your situation verbally with the person you authorize.

**Notice to Clients:** Most client information DSHS has is confidential and will not be disclosed to others unless you grant permission or if disclosure is allowed by law. After DSHS discloses your confidential information, please be aware that the recipient may not protect your records under the same laws that apply to DSHS. DSHS cannot refuse you benefits if you do not sign this form to allow disclosures to DSHS unless your authorization is needed to determine eligibility. For information on how DSHS health care components covered by HIPAA share protected health information and your privacy rights, please consult the DSHS Notice of Privacy Practices at www.dshs.wa.gov or ask the person who gave you this form. You may get a copy of this form.

**Use:** You may fill out this form electronically or by hand. Use the tab key on a computer to move between fields. **A separate form must be completed for each person whose records are requested, including children.** "You" refers to the subject of the records.

**Parts of Form:**

IDENTIFICATION OF SUBJECT OF RECORDS:
- Name: Provide your full name or the name of the person whose records are requested if you are acting for someone else.
- Date of birth: Please include this information needed to identify you from persons with similar names.

OPTIONAL INFORMATION to help locate records:
- Former names: Include any other names that have been used when receiving benefits or services.
- Client identification number: Provide any number that DSHS may have assigned.
- Other identification number: Include any other identifier that could help locate DSHS records. Only provide a social security number if necessary.
- Date and location of services: Provide this information to help DSHS identify and locate the records you want disclosed.

PERSON RECEIVING RECORDS:
- Identification: Please fill out this section as fully as possible so we can contact the person or organization who will have access to your confidential information.
- Reason for Disclosure: This information is required before DSHS can share drug and alcohol or mental health records. If you do not fill in this field, DSHS will note the reason for disclosure as being at your request.

AUTHORIZATION:
- Parts of DSHS: Please mark either the parts of DSHS you want to disclose records or mark the bottom box in this section if you want to give access to any records DSHS has about you. Write in the name of program in "Other" if not in the list.
- Information disclosed: Indicate what records that you want disclosed. You may allow disclosure of all or part of your DSHS client or other confidential records. You may also limit disclosure to client records held only by the parts of the agency marked in the section above, or to specific records listed on this form or on an attachment you sign. If there are any limitations on what records you want disclosed, either list specific records or describe the limits, such as by date of services or type of record.
- Restricted records: If any of the records may include information about HIV/AIDS or STD testing or treatment, mental health treatment, or drug and alcohol services, you must check each item to allow DSHS to disclose these records. You need to complete a separate form to authorize disclosure of psychotherapy notes (45 CFR 164.508(b) (3) (ii)).
- Validity: This form is valid to give access to information currently held by DSHS. Your permission expires 180 days after signature or on any other date or event you provide. If you do not provide a date, the authorization will be valid for 180 days. You may revoke the authority to release records in writing at any time but it will be too late to take back information already produced.
- Cost: The public records act in RCW 42.56.120 and WAC 388-01-080 allow DSHS to charge for copies of records plus mailing costs. State hospitals and health care facilities may charge for patient records under Chapter 70.02 RCW.

SIGNATURES:
- If you are the subject of the records, sign and also print or type your name below. Insert the date you signed plus your telephone or contact number.
- If you are signing for another person, indicate why you can do so on the last line and attach a copy of the court order or other document giving you legal authority. Children must also sign to give permission to disclose their own confidential records if they are over the age of consent (13 for mental health and drug and alcohol services; 14 for information about HIV/AIDS or other STDs; any age for birth control and abortions; 18 for health or other records).
- Witness or notary: A witness or notary may be needed to verify your identity if you do not submit this form in person or if a program requests verification. This person should sign and print his or her name.

---

NOTICE TO DSHS: If these records contain HIV or STD information, DSHS must notify recipients that the information is confidential and that they may not further disclose the records without a specific authorization as required by RCW 70.02.300. If DSHS sends copies of records regarding drug or alcohol services under this authorization, DSHS must include the following statement when disclosing information as required by 42 CFR 2.32:

> This information has been disclosed to you from records protected by Federal confidentiality rules (42 CFR part 2). The Federal rules prohibit you from making any further disclosure of this information unless further disclosure is expressly permitted by the written consent of the person to whom it pertains or as otherwise permitted by 42 CFR part 2. A general authorization for the release of medical or other information is NOT sufficient for this purpose. The Federal rules restrict any use of the information to criminally investigate or prosecute any alcohol or drug abuse patient.

## DADS Client Intake Form

### ABOUT THIS VISIT

Today's Date:_____

**DADS Location:** ☐ Seattle ☐ Lakewood ☐ BLH ☐ Progress House ☐ Pierce County Jail ☐ Other _____
**Services Needed:** ☐ Child Support ☐ Parenting Plan (Custody/Visitation) ☐ Guidance Coaching ☐ CPS Case ☐ Re-Entry Support ☐ Other _____
**Who Referred You?** ☐ Self ☐ Court ☐ Child Support ☐ Friend ☐ Family Member ☐ Other _____

### CLIENT INFORMATION

**First Name:** _____ **Middle:** _____ **Last Name:** _____
**Nickname/Goes By:** _____ **GENDER:** ☐ M ☐ F ☐ OTHER **Age:** _____
**Social Security Number:** ___-___-___ **Date of Birth:** ___-___-___
**Cell Phone:** ( ) ___-___ **Alternate:** ( ) ___-___ **Email:** _____
**Address:** _____ **Apt:** _____
**City:** _____ **State:** _____ **Zip Code:** _____

**Race or Ethnicity:** ☐ Black or African American ☐ American Indian or Alaska Native ☐ Asian or Asian American ☐ Hispanic or Latino ☐ Multi-Racial ☐ Hawaiian or Other Pacific Islander ☐ White or European ☐ Other _____
**Are you a refugee or immigrant?** ☐ Yes ☐ No **Are you homeless?** ☐ Yes ☐ No
**Marital Status:** ☐ Single ☐ Married ☐ Separated ☐ Divorced ☐ Widowed ☐ Other **Do you have a substance abuse issue?** ☐ Yes ☐ No ☐ In Recovery **Do you consider yourself a person with a disability?** ☐ Yes ☐ No

**Have you ever been incarcerated?** ☐ Yes ☐ No **If yes, which facility?** _____
**How long were you incarcerated?** _____ **When were you released?** ☐ >90 Days ☐ 90 Days or more
**Are you in work release?** ☐ Yes ☐ No **If yes, which facility?** _____

**Employment Status:** ☐ Employed ☐ Unemployed **Current Employer:** _____
**Source of Income:** ☐ Employment ☐ TANF ☐ GAU ☐ SSI/SSA/SSDI ☐ Unemployment Benefits ☐ Retirement
**Annual Income:** ☐ Less than $10,000 ☐ $10,000-$19,000 ☐ $20,000-$29,000 ☐ $30,000-$39,000 ☐ $40,000 +

### ABOUT YOUR CHILDREN

**Parental Relationship:** ☐ Custodial ☐ Non-Custodial **Are you currently seeing your children?** ☐ Yes ☐ No
**Number of Biological Children:** _____ **Number under 18:** _____ **Number living with you:** _____
**Have you established paternity or are you on the birth certificate?** ☐ Yes ☐ No ☐ I'm not sure
**Are you currently paying child support?** ☐ No ☐ Yes, I pay full $ _____ ☐ Yes, I pay partial $ _____
**How much in arrears or back child support do you think that you owe?** $_____

Please list all children below not just the ones you are here for.

**Name:** _____ **DOB:** ___/___/___ **Age:** _____ **Gender:** ☐ M ☐ F
**Name:** _____ **DOB:** ___/___/___ **Age:** _____ **Gender:** ☐ M ☐ F
**Name:** _____ **DOB:** ___/___/___ **Age:** _____ **Gender:** ☐ M ☐ F
**Name:** _____ **DOB:** ___/___/___ **Age:** _____ **Gender:** ☐ M ☐ F
**Name:** _____ **DOB:** ___/___/___ **Age:** _____ **Gender:** ☐ M ☐ F

# DADS Service Episode Record

☐ New Client  ☐ Returning Client        Today's Date: _____ / _____ / _____

First Name: _____ Last Name: _____ SSN: _____ - _____ - _____

**Any changes since clients last visit to DADS (phone number, address, child born, income, etc.):**
_____
_____
_____
_____
_____
_____

**Service Episode Notes (Why client came in, what was accomplished?):**
_____
_____
_____
_____
_____
_____
_____
_____
_____
_____
_____
_____
_____
_____
_____
_____

**Any Barriers for the client and next steps:**
_____
_____
_____
_____
_____
_____

# Divine Alternative for Dads Services Evaluation Form

On a scale from 1 (not at all satisfied) to 5 (very satisfied), how satisfied were you with this program?

    1        2        3        4        5

Not at all satisfied                    Very satisfied

On a scale from 1 (least valuable) to 5 (most valuable), how would you rate this program?

    1        2        3        4        5

Least valuable                    Most valuable

Share of your experience here today in a few sentences or less.

_____

_____

_____

_____

Thank you for sharing your opinions. We hope to have helped make a difference in your life.

## 1.5 Terms and Abbreviations

**Administrative Hearing:** Administrative hearings are "user-friendly" legal proceedings to resolve child support issues. An Administrative Law Judge holds the hearing usually by telephone and the attendees would be a representative from child support familiar with the modification request and the parties involved in the case. Each person involved in the case will get to state their case and the Judge will make a determination based on facts and findings within the guidelines of the law.

**Administrative Law Judge: (ALJ)** an official of a federal or state agency who hears, weighs, and decides on evidence in administrative proceedings, and makes recommendations for any necessary legal action.

**Administrative Order:** An order to pay child support that was established either through the Division of Child Support directly or through DSHS when a person is receiving public benefits such as TANF.

**Affidavit of Parentage: (AOP)** is a **voluntary signed admission of paternity made by the parents of a child**. This has the same legal effect as an order of paternity unless the admission of paternity is rescinded by either parent. This document must be signed by both parents in order for it to be admissible. By signing this form a man is waiving his rights to a genetic DNA test and assuming full legal and financial responsibility for the child. This form will also assist in attaching the father's name to a birth certificate.

**Arrears:** A debt that the non-custodial parent builds up as past due when they do not pay their current monthly child support obligation in full each month. This can be either to the custodial parent or to the state agency that the amount is due to. Another term for arrears is back child support.

**Arrears Payment:** A payment to the past due debt amount that is owed rather than the current amount due. If there is an excessive amount of arrears due, there is a possibility that DCS can include an additional amount into the current payment due to start recovering the arrears amount to help a case start to become current.

**Back Child Support:** See "Arrears" definition.

**Case Number:** Each child support case is assigned a case number to identify the case and all the logistics surrounding it such as payments due, payment history and parties involved in that particular case. Some non-custodial parents have more than one case number depending on the number of children they have and how many custodial parents that may be involved. Case numbers are labeled with **IV-D** which stands for **Title IV, Part D** of the Social Security Act of 1975.

**Case Payment History:** This is a record kept by DCS to show the current amount due, the amount that is in arrears, the case number history, whom the payment is assigned to and all parties involved.

**Child Protective Services: (CPS)** is a state agency that investigates reports of abuse and/or neglect against a child. Child safety is their first concern and they will work with both parents to ensure that a child is safely cared for. This agency is now a department within the Department of Children, Youth and Families (DCYF).

**Child Support: (CS)** is an order to pay support by the non-custodial parent to the custodial parent or to DSHS if owed. This can be an administrative order or a court order.

**Conference Board: (CB)** is an informal meeting to resolve CS problems EXCEPT changing the amount of current monthly CS due. The Conference Board Chair is a DCS attorney who makes the decisions based on facts and findings in the case. A conference board may release liens filed by DCS, release money DCS gets from bank accounts or IRS tax refunds, reduce the withholding from your pay, decide whether or not to report debt to a credit bureau, decide if DCS will enforce an order or collect a debt, reduce back support owed to the State of Washington, and review and correct other action taken by DCS.

**Court-Ordered Child Support:** A child support order that was set in court by a judge. This can happen as part of a divorce decree, a legal separation, or a parenting plan when child support is requested within. Court-ordered child support can only be changed through the courts. It is more difficult to request changes to court-ordered child support orders rather than an Administrative order. The Division of Child Support will track and manage all court-ordered child support payments, but they cannot make changes, only recommendations.

**Current (Payment):** this is the amount that is set for the non-custodial parent to pay each month in child support. This amount does not include any arrears payments that are due as those are additional debts incurred as a result of not staying current on child support obligations.

**Custodial Parent: (CP)** When parents are not living together, only one parent is considered the full legal custodian of the child(ren). That parent is the one that spends the most time with the children and is the one that is assigned to receive child support payments.

**Department of Social and Health Services: (DSHS)** provides different types of assistance to families in need such as cash, food, child support, child care, disability determination, transition to employment, medical, and other services depending on the situation.

**Division of Child Support: (DCS)** is a division of the Department of Social and Health Services responsible for the development and implementation of the rules, regulations, policies, and procedures necessary to ensure that all non-custodial parents are contributing to the economic support of their children.

**Division of Child Support Caseworker: (DCS Caseworker)** see "SEO" definition.

**Family Reconciliation Services: (FRS)** is a voluntary program serving runaway adolescents and youth in conflict with their families. The program targets adolescents between the ages of 12 through 17. FRS services are meant to resolve crisis situations and prevent unnecessary out of home placement. They are not long-term services. The services will assess and stabilize the family's situation. The goal is to return the family to a pre-crisis state and to work with the family to identify alternative methods of handling similar conflicts. If longer-term service needs are identified, FRS will help facilitate getting the youth and his/her family into on-going services.

**Lien:** A child support lien is a **hold placed on property** (such as land and cars) until past-due child support is paid. These liens will be placed without a court hearing. Liens must be paid off or released before the parent can sell the property.

**Non-Custodial Parent: (NCP)** is the parent that does not have primary physical custody of the child(ren). This is also the parent that is responsible for paying child support when and order is set forth.

**Office of Administrative Hearings: (OAH)** is an independent and impartial agency, which provides professional **administrative** law judges who are specially trained in **administrative** law to decide your kind of case.

**Petitioner:** The person that is initiating a legal action to take place in a court of law.

**Respondent:** This person is the additional party to a case filed and is in the position to respond to the initial filing.

**Support Enforcement Officer: (SEO)** Each person that either pays or receives child support is assigned a caseworker for their case. This person is their designated contact for any questions concerning their case.

**Temporary Assistance for Needy Families: (TANF)** This is a cash assistance program that provides help to pregnant women or clients that provide care for children and are in need.

**Waiver of Statute of Limitations: (Child-Support Related)** DCS can collect child support orders and arrearage judgments up to 10 years after the youngest child on the order turns 18. In some cases an NCP signed a Waiver of Statute of Limitations stating that they will be liable for the full debt amount regardless of the time lapse of the case. This means even if the debt is in arrears after the youngest child on the order turns 28, the NCP is still responsible for the debt until paid in full.

## 1.5.a Preparing for Incoming Call / Interview

1. Identify someone on your team as the "Client Intake Specialist." This person will receive all incoming calls.
2. It is important to have a notebook, or a stack of blank service episode forms, available to take notes for further use. Also, this can be used as part of the intake and engagement piece as you build a rapport with the client.
3. A standard greeting is appropriate to start the call: "Thank you for calling D.A.D.S. this is _____; how may I help you?"
4. When the client tells you his name, make sure to take note of it so you can update the interaction in Apricot (Note: We use Social Solutions Apricot software, a custom database software for small to mid-sized nonprofit organizations, with custom reporting and dashboards. You may use any database software you choose.)
5. Ask the client how he heard about D.A.D.S. and take note of this as well.
6. Listen intently to the caller and the main issue(s) they need resolved.
7. Check both Apricot (or your own database software) and ILINX (or your own CMS) while you are on the phone with the client, in case they already have an account open with D.A.D.S. and do not remember.
8. Allow the caller to tell their story but do not allow them to wander. Limit each phone call to no more than 15 minutes. Do this by advising the caller that if the subject matter of the call is parenting, custody, visitation, or child support modification, then the caller needs to schedule an appointment.
9. It is vital that the caller feels that they are being heard and taken seriously by the Client Intake Specialist. The Client Intake Specialist must "listen to the client with an open heart and prayer."
10. Do not be hasty to get the client off the phone with an email. Ask all the appropriate questions, depending on the situation. A client cannot do a parenting plan if that individual is not on the birth certificate; that is a good starting place of engagement.
11. Determine whether the is call related to parenting, custody, visitation, or child support modification. Anything to do with seeing their child(ren) is a parenting plan-related service need. Any mention of child support, financial hardship, etc. is a child support and parent education-related service need.
    **If child support is issue of concern, ask the caller to bring in:**
    - Income verification (pay stubs for past two months, tax returns for the last two years). If not available, bring what they have for verification
    
    **If parenting plan is issue of concern, ask the caller to bring in:**
    - Child(ren)'s birth certificate, existing divorce documents, protection or restraining order, or any court documents that involve the child(ren) or other parent

12. Before sending him the online intake forms, ask the client which office he would like to be seen in (for Washington State, this would be either the Seattle or Lakewood office).
13. When all steps have been followed, then send the email with the intake forms.
14. If the issue is child support and you have asked the appropriate questions, make sure you have the client's name, the date, and all service episode information filled out so that the service episode can be completed after the online intake is submitted.
15. When the issue is a parenting plan, or parenting plan related issues, still have the client call back in three to five days as you are still waiting on DCS for those issues. Continue your engagement by asking the appropriate questions and make them an appointment to come in to the closest office to continue their journey with D.A.D.S.

## 1.5.b Follow Through after Sending the Online Intake Forms; Making a Folder for Clients

1. Check for Online Intake Forms section in Apricot—or your database software program—daily. (Apply below instructions to whatever program you use, if not Apricot.)
2. When name of client shows up in Apricot under "Online Intake Forms," find name.
3. Scroll down and put in the "File Location" (hit), "Save Record" (hit), "Continue."
4. Print out the Client Intake Profile.
5. Print out the DSHS Form that is in Apricot under DSHS Authorization.
6. You should have a folder that already has "Intake Folder Checklist" attached to the left-hand side of folder.
7. When DSHS form is printed out, send it to DSHS.
8. Ask a co-worker to send it for you if you do not have access to this.
9. Record your interaction with the client on the "Service Episode Record."
10. Scan in all documents into ILINX.
11. Put all the information on the folder that is needed.
12. Put all the documents into the folder and into a proper filing cabinet (or, if you are keeping electronic copies, in the appropriate folder in ILINX).

# CHAPTER TWO

# 2.1 Child Support Assistance

If a mother or father comes in for child support assistance, there are several questions that can and should be asked to understand the client's case and to help them with their needs. When asking questions make sure that you make notes on the Service Episode Record as the father answers so that you can refer back to these when needed.

- How many biological children do you have? (You will also find the answer to this question on the bottom of the intake form for D.A.D.S.)
- What are the ages of the children? (This question is important to consider if the client has an old child support case and has since had a new baby that needs to be updated into the calculation.)
- What kind of help are you looking for when it comes to your child support case?
- Is your child support case out of Washington State or another state? (Every state is different when it comes to its policies and procedures.)
- Are you currently employed and are you making more or less money now than you did when your child support order was established? (Making substantially less income could possibly assist our client's claim to want to modify his/her current order.)
- Do you have back child support due, or what is referred to as arrears?
- Have you been incarcerated since the child support order has been in place? Did your back child support build up while you were incarcerated?
- Are you currently paying your full child support obligation or just the state-required monthly minimum? Are your paychecks being garnished by DCS?
- Are you disabled and receiving disability benefits?
- What is the current residential schedule of the children; were they living with the mother when the order was created and now reside with the father?
- Has the mother ever received public assistance from the state?

- Are you paying the mother directly out of pocket or is there an order through DCS or the court system?

Scenarios when it pertains to child support based on the above questions.

1. Randy comes into D.A.D.S. feeling defeated that he isn't able to survive with the income he is bringing home after child support is deducted from his checks. He is going to lose his place and will soon be homeless. He doesn't understand why they are able to garnish his checks for so much money when he is only making minimum wage. Randy's children are ages seven and nine and by one mother. Randy made $80,000 a year when the original child support order was created through DCS (not a court order). What information would you share with Randy?
    a. You would want to clarify with Randy that he is making the support payments as ordered and suggest to him that he contact child support directly as they are more willing to work with someone who is trying. (Also refer to section 2.2 for modification assistance.)
    b. Explain to the client that DCS is allowed to take up to 50 percent of his paycheck after taxes are deducted for child support. It sounds like he has some child support that is in arrears and hasn't been able to make his monthly support obligations. We would need to have a DCS Authorization submitted and wait to review it once it has been returned to us to further assist the client. This would also fall in line with requesting a modification (Refer to section 2.2 for assistance.)
    c. Randy will start by calling DCS to see if he can make any arrangements with them first. Then, if he wants to proceed with a modification, he will return to do that. Randy will also call in a few days to review the DCS documentation that we have received to see if there is anything that can be done to further assist him with his child support case.
2. Shantelle comes into D.A.D.S. and requests help with getting her child support lowered, saying that she currently isn't working and is going to school full time for cosmetology so that she can one day work in a salon. She is ordered to pay $500 per month for her son, who is living with his father. She hasn't paid child support in almost a year and doesn't feel she needs to be responsible for child support while in school and unemployed. She doesn't want to seek employment at this time because she is afraid they will take all of her paychecks for child support and she wants to put her focus on her schooling. What information would you share with Shantelle?
    a. The Division of Child Services assumes the non-custodial parent will be working full time and they calculate the payment in that way. Being a full-time college

student does not exempt you from paying child support; however, you may be able to speak with your case worker to see if you can work out a payment plan in the meantime.
b. Suggest to Shantelle to obtain employment around her school hours even if it is only part-time work. Let Shantelle know that the child support obligation will continue to build into arrears and she will be digging a bigger hole when she obtains full-time employment in her career choice. Also explain to Shantelle that DCS can take up to 50 percent of her paycheck after taxes if she goes into garnishment, so the best thing to do is to get a handle on her child support obligations now.
c. Shantelle will start by calling her DCS case worker first to see if she can make any arrangements on her case. Once she obtains steady employment, we can refer to section 2.2 to possibly assist her with a modification to her case.

## 2.2 Administrative vs. Court-Ordered

**Administrative Order of Child Support:** This would be a child support order that was established either through the Division of Child Support directly or through DSHS when a person is receiving public benefits such as TANF. This order can also be established if a child has gone into the foster care system as well or CPS placement.

**Court-Ordered Child Support:** This is a child support order that was set in court by a judge. This can happen as part of a divorce decree, a legal separation, or a parenting plan when child support is requested within. Court-ordered child support can only be changed through the courts. It is more difficult to request changes to court-ordered child support orders rather than an Administrative Order. The Division of Child Support will track and manage all court-ordered child support payments, but they cannot make changes, only recommendations.

**Interstate Collection of Child Support:** This type of order originates in a state other than the State of Washington. Washington is only collecting on behalf of the state in which the order is in place. Any and all requests for changes or for a modification inquiry must go directly through the originating state.

### 2.2a Modifications

When a parent comes in and requests help with their child support case and would like a modification, you would first need to determine what type of case they have. If it is an Interstate Collection of Child Support, you would refer them to the originating Division of Child Support Agency.

## Administrative Order

The parent must submit a separate request for each child support order that he wants to modify. Child support orders less than a year old are rarely granted a modification without adequate cause. Child support orders older than one year can be modified when there is a change of circumstance. Some examples below are good reasons for a request to modify an order:

- Incarceration
- Individual has become disabled and is now receiving disability benefits
- Recently went on public assistance and is receiving TANF
- A new biological child was born into the home
- An additional child was added to create a new child support order
- New employment with a lower income than previously reported
- Previous childcare payment through DCS; however, the child(ren) are no longer receiving childcare
- The child(ren) are now in your care more than half time

Once we have helped to determine that the client is eligible to try and modify their child support case, we have them bring in documentation and help them to fill out the Petition for Modification form that can be found on the DCS website. It is up to them to take it down to DCS or to mail it in, but they must have all of the required documentation or the case will be thrown out and they will have to start over.

## Court-Ordered

For court-ordered child support cases, we are able to contact DCS to see what exactly the client needs to do to start the process, but ultimately the client will have to go through the prosecutor's office to get the modification started. The case must be at least two years old from the date the order was put in place or one year from the date a case is opened if the child turns 12 from the date of the order. The child support website does provide a list of forms that will be needed to assist the client with a court-ordered modification if you would like to refer them to there to start the process. The only way that DCS can assist with a court-ordered child support case is if the custodial parent signs up for public assistance.

## 2.2.b Arrears

This is also known as back child support and is created when a non-custodial parent is unable to make their full monthly payment each month as set forth in either an administrative order or a court order. This can also be an amount that is in addition to a current monthly amount set on an order, for instance, if a person is ordered $300 per month on a current order and ordered to pay an additional back payment amount of $5000, that amount will go into arrears to be paid.

When the arrears amount goes over $2,500, DCS can:

- Raise the current amount due each month to apply payments towards the arrears amount.
- Suspend any license that the non-custodial parent may have (drivers, professional, liquor, fishing, hunting, etc.)
- Place a hold on a passport.
- Seize money that is in bank accounts attached to one's social security number or tax returns.
- Put a lien on properties owned such as land or vehicles.
- Post the case to the DCS Most Wanted website (this is done at the request of the custodial parent)
- As a last resort, if DCS is unable to collect, the case can be referred to the Prosecutor's Office for review and judicial enforcement. This could lead to jail time if the non-custodial parent is noncompliant.

Arrears debt will follow an individual until the case is 10 years beyond the last child turning 18 or the case closing. In most cases that would mean that the debt will fall off when the youngest child on the order turns 28. There are exceptions to this if a judge in a court-ordered child support case places a different stipulation on the arrears or if there was a Waiver of the Statute of Limitations signed.

# CHAPTER THREE

# 3.1 Parenting Plan Assistance

A parenting plan is an agreement to decide the rights of each parent when it comes to the children. Included in the parenting plan will also be the visitation schedule for the non-custodial parent as well as the decision making between the parents when it comes to the children's daily and extracurricular needs. A parenting plan is meant to help the parents align a schedule when it comes to taking care of the children when a civil agreement cannot be obtained. We encourage families to try and work out an agreement without going through the courts as the judge does not know the children or the parents and if an agreement can't be made through the process, then the judge will make the final order for the children.

When a non-custodial parent comes in and requests help with custody, visitation, or uses the term "Parenting Plan," it is important to clarify to them that we are not lawyers. We do not work with any lawyers and we will not appear in court with them. We are here to give suggestions and guidance to the best of our ability and to give the parent the tools to walk through the process on their own. Our suggestions are just suggestions based on our own knowledge and gained experience, and are not meant to be legal advice. Also, we will not fill out the forms for an individual; if they want to be involved in their child's life, they will do the work. We are here to help them and give them the next steps to take in their journey.

Exploring the wants, needs and requests of the father can help you to understand if a parenting plan should even be used or if you need to focus on another avenue of assistance to the client. Below are some important questions to ask the client and some key points to look for before starting a parenting plan:

1. **What is the relationship with the other parent?**
    a. When did the two of you split up? Is this a recent event? If the break up/separation is fairly new, give time for the air to clear and for both parties to cool down. Explain that there is a strong possibility that the two of them can work things out for the best interest of the children without a court battle. Ask how the relationship was before the break up with regard to the decision-making for the children. Chances are, with clear communication and putting the children first, co-parenting can be established without a parenting plan.
    b. Does either parent have a new significant other in their lives and is this causing mixed feelings and affecting the way co-parenting has been done up to this point? Encourage the positive side of what is in the best interest of the children and how important it is to have an open line of communication with all parties involved. It's important for the children to see that both parents are able to get along in any situation. Suggest a possible sit down with the parents and significant others and try to come together as a team and set boundaries with co-parenting. Explain that a judge does not want to hear he said/she said and will not be a referee.
    c. Does it sound like there is a retaliation situation going on or some anger issues causing conflict? These might be some issues that need to be addressed first before proceeding to a parenting plan. It's important to counsel the client about the importance of keeping a positive relationship with the other parent and setting an example for them. Possibly invite the client to join the men's group in either office to get a clear mind and some guidance before proceeding.
2. **Are there concerns about the welfare of the children?**
    a. Are there disagreements about the different parenting styles between the two households? Is a new relationship involving either parent, leading to arguments, but these issues are not causing harm or putting the children at risk? This would be a good time to redirect the client to focus his attention more on critical issues and what is best for the children. Creating a more positive relationship with the other parent will help the children in their upbringing. Sometimes, in this case, a parenting plan may be best to set boundaries, but explain that a judge isn't going to set unreasonable expectations of one parent towards another.
    b. Do you feel that there is an imminent danger clue when it comes to the children's health and safety? Are there concerns of abuse or neglect that are clear to be seen? The last thing you want to do is claim abuse out of anger or a different parenting style and see the case be thrown out as fraud and untrue. Is there

suspected drug use in the home or by the other parent? Has the custodial parent been in and out of jail while caring for the children, or living with a sexual offender? If the custodial parent is living with a felon, this doesn't necessarily ring alarms for abuse; people make mistakes and our judicial system is set up to reprimand someone for those mistakes. Just because someone is a felon doesn't determine grounds for abuse, neglect, or danger for a child. If the parent feels that their child(ren) are seriously in danger, we suggest that they contact CPS and ask for their recommendations. If CPS investigates the other parent and makes a report to change guardianship from one parent to the other, D.A.D.S. can help with the parenting plan. The parent will need to attach that documentation to the declaration section and reference "according to CPS recommendations."
   c. Is there a concern that the children are not eating regularly, bathing regularly, or getting the medical or dental care that they need? Is this perhaps due to a different parenting style or a lack of parenting? Are the children being left alone at an inappropriate age or with someone you feel is unsafe? Have you tried to address these concerns with the other parent to try to come to a positive solution? Have you volunteered to parent the children on the hours that the other parent is using a sitter that you feel is unsafe and you are available?
3. **What is your relationship like with your child(ren)?**
   a. Do you see your children regularly? Do you call them regularly? If not, a starting point wouldn't be to ask for full custody from the very start. Explain that a judge is going to look for the best interest of the children and getting to know them is a starting place. Remember that something is better than nothing and the parenting plan can always be changed once you make an effort to become active within your children's lives.
   b. Have you been seeing the children regularly and right now there is some conflict between you and the other parent? We would suggest that you avoid the time, expense, and process of going through a court to determine the children's time. If you and the other parent can come to any kind of terms, at least it's a start. It is something as you build on the nurturing relationship with your children. As they get older, they will ask for more time with you, and with you being available to the other parent, they will ask for more help. Communication is the key; take what you can get and build with that. If you are seeing your children four days a week now and decide a parenting plan is best, what happens when a judge only gives you every other weekend? This can happen. Do you want the lesser time allotted for your children, or to try and work things out on your own?

4. **The children do not want to live with the other parent.**
   a. Have the children asked to live with you because the other parent is unloving, angry, or unsupportive? Is one parent the "fun" weekend parent and one parent the discipline source? These are not reasons to overturn custody of children from one parent to another. Also, when children become teenagers, they are going to almost always test their boundaries between parents. It's important to support one another and the decision-making for the children. If one parent says a child is grounded for the weekend, the other parent should support that as long as it isn't taking away the other parent's time. Try to come to an agreement with the other parent and show the child that you are all on the same page, and you might get a different reaction. If you feel that there is serious harm or extreme stress, then, yes, maybe a parenting plan with request for the majority of residential time may be best. Remember, though, without proof and cause, a judge isn't going to remove a child from a home where they have been thriving and cared for, just because they don't want to follow the rules and want a more lax environment.

There are certain key phrases that you will need to look for when a non-custodial parent comes in to request a parenting plan or looking for full custody of their children. Be straightforward with the client and with what they need to do based on what you are hearing rather than to be quick to adhere to their requests.

1. **He doesn't talk about his relationship with his kids; all you hear about is the mother.**
   a. Ask him about the relationship with his children. It's okay to be up front that you haven't heard anything about the children and all you have heard is the mom did this and the mom did that. Let him know that it seems as if his purpose is to win a battle against the mom, and that a judge will see right through that in court. Counsel him that he needs to redirect his anger towards the mom into building a healthy relationship with his children. Suggest to him that he needs to make an effort to get along with the mother and take small steps to seeing his children and opening lines of communication without the negative and conflict. Explain to him that if he goes into court with the approach that he is taking, a judge could order him supervised visits. These are expensive and, depending on his anger, he could possibly end up with a no contact/restraining order. It will be much easier to let go of the hurt and pain from the failed relationship and focus his energy on building with his children. He has to start somewhere and invite him to the men's group.

2. **The father works long hours, or doesn't have a job at all or a place of his own.**
    a. If you hear that the father is working long hours and the children will spend most of their visitation scheduled time in the care of someone else or alone depending on the age, encourage him to request time that he is actually available to the children.
    b. Unless disabled, suggest to the father that he obtain full-time employment and work on establishing a place of his own. This will show his stability to the court and he will more than likely get his requested visitation with this in place.
3. **There is a history of arrest and/or incarceration for violent crimes and domestic violence.**
    a. For any client, male or female, who walks into D.A.D.S., it is pertinent that they are following the current stipulations or court-ordered requirements that are in place. If they have this history, the judge will want to see what steps they have made to change and to prove that they want to be a part of their children's lives. It may be better for them to take another route, if at all possible, rather than going to court because the criminal history can be used against them. With this criminal history, they can be ordered to attend domestic violence classes or even assigned a protection order within the parenting plan, as well as supervised visits. If they adhere to all stipulations, they can later modify the parenting plan to show that they are serious about being a good parent.
4. **There is an addiction or they are currently in treatment for an addiction.**
    a. If a client comes in and is showing signs of addiction, or is possibly intoxicated at the time, ask if they have a problem with drugs or alcohol. We are not here to cast judgment, only to provide our clients with the help and support they need, to the best of our abilities.
    b. If the client says they are currently in treatment, congratulate them and encourage them to completely focus on their sobriety for right now. It's the best thing that they can do for their children and this will also show progress to the judge. Suggest that the client come back when they have been out of treatment and sober for at least six months, and have steady employment and a place of their own. Once they start the parenting plan process, they will want to show stability.
    c. If the client says yes, encourage them to seek treatment first before starting a parenting plan. They need to focus on taking care of themselves and becoming healthy and sober before we can proceed with helping them to request time with their children. They most likely will not want to hear this, but it is what is best for the children.

d.  If the client says no, make sure that they have provided the birth certificate of the children that they are there to seek visitation for first, and then just hand them the parenting plan to fill out at home. Do not offer assistance except when they return it; this will give them a chance to show that they can complete a task and that they are serious for the help.

Working out visitation between the parents is the best route to take unless there is absolutely no way to communicate effectively. Explain to the client that not only does it take up to a year for a parenting plan to be finalized; there are classes and court dates in between time. They have to be prepared to pay court fees, unless they qualify for a waiver, but they will miss work and time to attend scheduled case setting dates as well. The end result could go either way, there are no guarantees that they will get what they are requesting. The judge will hear both sides and make the final decision based on the facts and findings presented to them.

If the client still would like to proceed with the parenting plan, instruct them to obtain a copy of the child's birth certificate to continue. They have to be listed on the birth certificate or have a copy of the signed Affidavit of Parentage in order to file a parenting plan in the State of Washington.

# 3.2 Establishing Parentage

There are four primary ways to establish parentage. Once established, the father's name can be added to the child's birth certificate.

1. **Marriage**: If the mother and biological father are married before the child is born, the marriage may create what is called a presumption of parentage. Unless a parent or some other interested party later challenges that presumption, the man will be considered to be the legal father of the child.
2. **Registered Domestic Partnership**: If the mother was in a registered domestic partnership during the pregnancy, the registered domestic partnership may create what is called a presumption of parentage. Unless a parent or some other interested party later challenges that presumption, the registered domestic partner is considered the legal parent of the child.
3. **Court Order**: The court may determine if a person is the legal parent of a child by a required genetic test of the mother, child, and the alleged father. Upon positive testing results, the court will enter an order and the birth certificate can accurately be amended to show the biological father to be listed.
4. **Acknowledgement of Parentage**: This form when signed by both the mother and the presumed father is a legal binding contract. By signing this form, the "father" is agreeing that he: 1) is the biological father, 2) is waiving his rights to a DNA genetic test, and 3) agrees to be financially responsible for the child in the future if the mother ever applies for state benefits or child support.

## Scenarios

1. Jacob comes in and wants assistance with creating a parenting plan; however, his name is not on the birth certificate. In order to file a parenting plan with the courts, this is a requirement. What would you instruct Jacob to do?

a. If he believes that the child is his without any doubt and he gets along with the mother, you can refer him to either print the form off online and they both complete the form. Or, in Washington State, they can go down to the Center for Health Statistics (located in Tumwater, Washington) to do it in person. The most important thing to remember when signing this form is that it is binding with a small window of time for either party to rescind their signature (within 60 days after the form is signed). This form needs either a witness aged 18 or older and not related by blood or marriage to the parties that are signing the form, or it can be notarized.
b. Jacob can file a Petition to Decide Parentage through the Superior Court of the county where the child is residing. Jacob would be responsible for the filing fees as well as the genetic testing fees. He could possibly request a waiver for the filing fees depending on his income.
c. You can refer Jacob to go to the Division of Child Support and request to be put on child support and to have DNA established. If the DNA test comes back that Jacob is the father, DCS will not charge him for the cost of the DNA test; however, if the test comes back that he is not the father, he will be responsible for the cost of the test.
d. There is also a program through DCS called the Voluntary Paternity Testing Program; this program is supposed to be free of charge with no risk of being placed on child support, but both the mother and father have to agree to paternity testing. There is a form that needs to be filled out and mailed in and then a DCS representative will contact both parties to schedule the test.
2. Steven wants to know why he is on the birth certificate and he didn't sign the Acknowledgement of Paternity form and never had a DNA test done. How could this be?
a. If the mother opens a DCS case, or applies for state assistance such as TANF, she is required to name three men that she believes may be the father of the child in order to receive benefits. Each man will be given an opportunity to respond and take a DNA test to prove (or disprove) parentage of the child. If a man does not respond and does not agree to take the DNA test, he can be made the father by default.
3. Chase is worried that his child will be lost in the foster care system as the mother of his newborn child was addicted to drugs and the child was born with drugs in their system. What suggestion would you make for Chase?

a. Have Chase immediately contact the CPS Social Worker involved with the case. The CPS worker will have a DNA test ordered and if Chase is the biological father, his name can and will be placed on the birth certificate.
b. Also, have Chase make sure he works with CPS and DCS in getting placement of the child into his care after the genetic testing comes back in his favor and he is determined to be the biological father of the child.
c. Explain to Chase that this situation isn't a cake walk to getting his child in his care; he will be required to jump through some hoops. If he is serious about wanting to step up as a father and take care of his child, he needs to comply with all the steps requested by CPS.

## 3.3 Developing a Parenting Plan

The following instructions and forms are subject to change depending on the court case schedule or when new/expired laws are set into motion. This is just a guide to help a client through the process; they are required to fill out the paperwork on their own as well as file it in the county where the child resides. It is also up to the client to have the other party served; we cannot participate in that step of the parenting plan either. We are here to guide, give suggestions, and review the parenting plan process to help the client through their journey of reconnecting with their children.

These forms are in the order that we know best and not necessarily the order that the courts would like. The clerk will separate everything when a client files them and put them in the order as they would like them to go. When filling out the following forms below, the "petitioner" is the person establishing the initial court procedure and the "respondent" is the other party to respond. It is important to make sure when reviewing a client's parenting plan that they have every question filled in with a response. (See Section 3.3d for an example of what a completed parenting plan should look like.)

### 3.3a Temporary Parenting Plan

It can take up to a year for a final parenting plan to be approved through the court process if the parents cannot come to an agreement before then. Part of the parenting plan package includes a temporary parenting plan so that the non-custodial parent can request visitation or custody while in the process of waiting for a final order. When the non-custodial parent is requesting time in the temporary parenting plan, make sure they are asking for a time that they can physically be with the child and not time the child will spend with a sitter or family member (unless the request is due to a CPS case or the police removal of the child, then that would require custody on a full-time basis to be requested).

## 3.3b Modification of a Parenting Plan

Once a parenting plan is finalized, it is best to give it some time before a parent requests a modification. In some cases, it is a good idea to follow the court's stipulations such as classes, assessments, and supervised visitations before requesting any type of modification to show that the client has made progress.

## 3.3c Case Schedule

At the time a family law petition is filed, the clerk shall issue a case schedule. The case schedule contains a list of mandatory deadlines. Failure to comply with the case schedule may result in sanctions or dismissal. A case schedule can sometimes change depending on different factors. It is important to not only follow the case schedule, but to also periodically call the clerk and make sure the case schedule that you have is up to date.

## 3.3d Example of a Completed Parenting Plan

The following pages are examples of the documentation that make up a parenting plan/temporary parenting plan (both will be submitted at the same time). These are provided as samples only; these forms may differ in different counties and states.

**Superior Court of Washington, County of** _____

In re:

Petitioner/s *(person/s who started this case)*:

_____

And Respondent/s *(other party/parties)*:

_____

No. _____

Notice of Hearing
(NTHG)

☒ Clerk's action required: **1**

# Notice of Hearing

**To the Court Clerk and all parties:**

**1.** A court hearing has been scheduled:

for: _____ at: _____ ☐ a.m. ☐ p.m.
     *date*                                   *time*

at: _____ in _____
    *court's address*                        *room or department*

_____
*docket / calendar or judge / commissioner's name*

**2.** The purpose of this hearing is *(specify)*:_____

***Warning!*** If you do not go to the hearing, the court may sign orders without hearing your side.

This hearing was requested by: ☐ Petitioner or his/her lawyer ☐ Respondent or his/her lawyer

▶ _____  _____  _____
*Person asking for this hearing signs here*  *Print name (if lawyer, also list WSBA #)*  *Date*

I agree to accept legal papers for this case at:

_____
*address*

_____
*city*        *state*     *zip*

**(Optional)** email: _____

This does **not** have to be your home address. If this address changes before the case ends, you **must** notify all parties and the court clerk in writing. You may use the *Notice of Address Change* form (FL All Family 120). A party must also update his/her *Confidential Information* form (FL All Family 001) if this case involves parentage or child support.

Optional Form *(05/2016)*
**FL All Family 185**

## KING COUNTY SUPERIOR COURT
## CASE ASSIGNMENT AREA DESIGNATION and CASE INFORMATION COVER SHEET
## (CICS)

Pursuant to King County Code 4A.630.060, a faulty document fee of $15 may be assessed to new case filings missing this sheet.

**CASE NUMBER:** _____
(Provided by the Clerk)

**CASE CAPTION:** _____
(New case: Print name of person starting case **vs.** name of person or agency you are filing against.)
(When filing into an existing family law case, the case caption remains the same as the original filing.)

Please mark one of the boxes below:

☐ **Seattle Area**, defined as:

> All of King County north of Interstate 90 and including all of the Interstate 90 right-of-way; all the cities of Seattle, Mercer Island, Bellevue, Issaquah and North Bend; and all of Vashon and Maury Islands.

☐ **Kent Area,** defined as:

> All of King County south of Interstate 90 except those areas included in the Seattle Case Assignment Area.

I certify that this case meets the case assignment criteria, described in King County LCR 82(e).

_____    _____
Signature of Attorney    WSBA Number    Date

or

_____    _____
Signature of person who is starting case    Date

_____
Address, City, State, Zip Code of person who is starting case if not represented by attorney

**KING COUNTY SUPERIOR COURT**
**CASE ASSIGNMENT AREA DESIGNATION and CASE INFORMATION COVER SHEET**

Definitions:
    Divorce/Dissolution -- married couples
    Paternity/Parentage --unmarried parents
    Dependent Children – generally under 18 years of age

## FAMILY LAW
Please check the category that best describes this case.

☐ Adoption (ADP 5)
(Petition to establish a new, permanent relationship of parent and child not having that relationship.)

☐ Annulment/Invalidity of Marriage
    ☐ with dependent children (INC 3)*
    ☐ without children (INV 3) *
    ☐ wife pregnant (INC 3)*
(Petition claiming an illegal or invalid marriage.)

☐ Annulment/Invalidity of Domestic Partnership
    ☐ with dependent children (IND 3)*
    ☐ without children (INP 3) *
    ☐ a partner is pregnant (IND 3)*
(Petition to invalidate a domestic partnership.)

☐ Challenge to Acknowledgment of Parentage (PAT 5)*
(Petition must be filed more than 60 days but less than two years after the Acknowledgment of Paternity was filed with the Washington State Registrar of Vital Statistics.)

☐ Committed Intimate Relationship
No Children (CIR 3)*
(Petition for distribution of property from a marital-like relationship where both parties cohabit with knowledge that a lawful marriage between them does not exist.)

☐ Confidential Intermediary (CFI 5)
(Petition to appoint a confidential intermediary to contact the adopted person(s), birth parent(s), or other relative(s).)

☐ Divorce
    ☐ with dependent children (DIC 3)*
    ☐ without children (DIN 3) *
    ☐ wife pregnant (DIC 3)*
(Petition to terminate a marriage other than annulment. Check an option below.)

☐ Divorce - Domestic Partnership
    ☐ with dependent children (DPC 3)*
    ☐ without children (DPN 3) *
    ☐ a partner is pregnant (DPC 3)*
(Petition to terminate a domestic partnership, other than annulment. Must have a Certificate number issued by the State where registered.)

Family Law CICS 01/2021

- ☐ Enforcement/Show Cause-Out of County (MSC 3)
- ☐ Enforcement of Open Adoption Agreement (OAA 5)*
- ☐ Establish Parenting Plan-includes CIR with Children (PPS 3)*
  (Petition for establishing Residential Schedule/Parenting Plan/Child Support in circumstances set forth in RCW 26.26.375.)
- ☐ Establish Parenting Plan (MSC 5)*
  (For existing King County Paternity case only.)
- ☐ Establish Support Only (PPS 3)*
  (There is no support order and paternity is not an issue.)
- ☐ Initial Pre-Placement Report (PPR 5)
  (An initial pre-placement report filed on a child by the DSHS prior to the filing of adoption papers.)
- ☐ Legal Separation (SEP 3)*
  - ☐ with dependent children (SEC 3)*
  - ☐ without children (SEP 3) *
  - ☐ wife pregnant (SEC 3)*
  (Petition to live separate and apart, but still married.)
- ☐ Legal Separation of Domestic Partnership
  - ☐ with dependent children (SDC 3)*
  - ☐ without children (SPD 3) *
  - ☐ a partner is pregnant (SDC 3)*
  (Petition to live separate and apart, in a domestic partnership.)
- ☐ Mandatory Wage Assignment (MWA 3)
  (A legal procedure that requires the employer to transfer parts of future wage payments to pay a debt.)

- ☐ Modification-Parenting Plan (may also include support)
  - ☐ Existing Divorce case(MOD 3)*
  - ☐ Existing Paternity case (MOD 5) *
  (Petition to seeking changes of Custody Decree, Parenting Plan/Residential Schedule of a previous order or decree.)
- ☐ Modification-Support Only
  - ☐ Existing Divorce case (MDS 3)*
  - ☐ Existing Paternity case (MDS 5) *
  (Petition seeking changes of a previous order or decree regarding support.)
- ☐ Out-of-State Custody Order Registration (OSC 3)
  (Recording custody established out-of-state.)
- ☐ Out-of-state Support Court Order Registration (FJU 3)
  (Recording support or maintenance established out-of-state.)
- ☐ Parentage, Disestablish (DIP 5)*
  (Disestablish parentage when there is no adjudicated father or acknowledgment of paternity filed with the Washington State Registrar of Vital Statistics.)
- ☐ Parentage/UIFSA (PUR 5)*
  (Petition to determine the legal status of a parent which is filed in conjunction with the reciprocal report entered under the URESA or UIFSA acts.)
- ☐ Paternity-Parental Determination (PAT 5)*
  (Petition to establish or determine the existence of parental relationship with the child.)
- ☐ Petition for de Facto Parentage (PAD 5)*
- ☐ Petition to Decide Parentage – Genetic Surrogacy Agreement (PAG 5)*

Family Law CICS 01/2021

☐ Petition to Decide Parentage – Gestational Surrogacy or Assisted Reproduction (PAS 5)*

☐ Relative Child Visitation (RCV 3)*
(Petition to allow grandparents and other relatives the ability to seek an order regarding visits with a child)

☐ Relinquishment (REL 5)
(Petition to relinquish a child to DSHS, an agency, or a prospective adoptive parent.)

☐ Relocation, Objection (ROB 3)

☐ Existing Divorce case(ROB 3)*
☐ Existing Paternity case (ROB 5)*
(Petition objecting to the intended relocation of the child or the relocating parent's proposed revised residential schedule.)

☐ Termination of Parent-Child Relationship (TER 5)
(Petition to terminate a parent-child relationship when parent has not executed a written consent.)

\* The filing party will be given an appropriate case schedule at time of filing.

Family Law CICS 01/2021

**SUPERIOR COURT OF WASHINGTON FOR PIERCE COUNTY**
**CASE COVER SHEET / CIVIL CASE**

Case Title_____  Case Number_____
Atty/Litigant_____  Bar#_____ Phone_____
Address_____   Email address_____
City_____ State_____  Zip Code_____

Please check one category that best describes this case for indexing purposes.
*If you cannot determine the appropriate category, Please describe the cause of action below. This will create a Miscellaneous cause which is not subject to PCLR 3.*

**APPEAL / REVIEW**
___Administrative Law Review (ALR 2) REV 6
___Civil, Non-Traffic (LCA 2) REV 6
___Civil, Traffic (LCI 2) REV 6
___Land Use Petition (LUP 2) LUPA
___DOL Revocation – Appeal (DOL) REV 4

**CONTRACT / COMMERCIAL**
___Breach of Contract, Commercial Non-Contract or Commercial-Contract (COM 2) STANDARD
___Third Party Collection (COL 2) REV 4
___Contractor Bond Complaint (CBC) REV 4

**JUDGEMENT**
___Judgement, Another County or Abstract Only (ABJ 2) Non PCLR
___Transcript of Judgement (TRJ 2) Non PCLR
___Foreign Judgement Civil or Judgement, Another State (FJU 2) Non PCLR

**TORT / MOTOR VEHICLE**
___Death, Non-Death Injuries or Property Damage Only (TMV 2) STANDARD

**TORT / NON MOTOR VEHICLE**
___Other Malpractice (MAL 2) COMPLEX
___Personal Injury (PIN 2) STANDARD

___Property Damage (PRP 2) STANDARD
___Wrongful Death (WDE 2) STANDARD
___Other Tort, Products Liability or Asbestos (TTO 2) COMPLEX

**PROPERTY RIGHTS**
___Condemnation (CON 2) STANDARD
___Foreclosure (FOR 2) REV 4
___Property Fairness (PFA 2) STANDARD
___Quiet Title (QTI 2) STANDARD
___Unlawful Detainer / Eviction (UND 2) REV 4
___Unlawful Detainer / Contested (UND 2) REV 4
___Unlawful Detainer Commercial (UNDB) REV 4

**OTHER COMPLAINT OR PETITION**
___Compel/Confirm Bind Arbitration, Deposit of Surplus Funds, Interpleader, Subpoenas, Victims' Employment Leave, or Wireless Number Disclosure, Miscellaneous (MSC 2) REV 4
___Injunction (INJ 2) REV 4
___Ballot Title (BAT) REV 4
___Subdivision Elect Law Review (SER) REV 4
___Minor Settlement/No Guardianship (MST2) REV 4
___Pet for Civil Commit/Sex Predator (PCC2) REV 4
___Property Damage Gangs (PRG 2) REV 4
___Relief from Duty to Register (RDR) REV 12
___Restoration of Firearm Rights (RFR 2) REV 4
___Seizure of Property/Comm. of Crime (SPC2) REV 4
___Seizure of Property Result from Crime (SPR2) REV 4
___Trust/Estate Dispute Resolution (TDR2) REV 12
___Restoration of Opportunity (CRP) REV 4
___Voter Election Law Review (VEP) REV 4
___Abusive Litigation (ABL) REV 4

**TORT / MEDICAL MALPRACTICE**
___Hospital, Medical Doctor, or Other Health Care Professional (MED2) COMPLEX

**WRIT**
___Habeas Corpus (WHC 2) REV 4
___Mandamus (WRM 2) REV 4
___Review (WRV 2) REV 4
___Miscellaneous Writ (WMW 2) REV 4

**MISCELLANEOUS**_____

**King County**
Superior Court Clerk's Office

## INSTRUCTIONS FOR
## MOTION AND ORDER TO WAIVE FILING FEES – KENT LOCATION

If you believe that you are unable to afford the civil fee and related surcharges in your civil or family law court case, you may request that the court waive it. In determining whether the filing fee should be waived, the Court will consider your ability to pay. In doing so, the court may apply a financial availability table based on 125% of the Federal Poverty Standard (see below). If there is a joint petition in a family law matter, your income will be added to your spouse's income in determining eligibility for a fee waiver.

However, the court may also waive the requirement for you to pay fees if your income is above the thresholds below, but finds that you have recurring basic living expenses which render you unable to pay the fees, or it may waive the fees if it finds there are other compelling circumstances to do so. If you are represented by a Qualified Legal Services Provider, that provider may obtain a fee waiver by presentation of the forms designated for their use.

| Family Size | 1 | 2 | 3 | 4 | 5 | 6 | 7 | 8 | 9 or more |
|---|---|---|---|---|---|---|---|---|---|
| Maximum Monthly Income* | $1,329 | $1,796 | $2,263 | $2,729 | $3,196 | $3,663 | $4,129 | $4,596 | Add $467 for each additional |
| Maximum Annual Income* | $15,950 | $21,550 | $27,150 | $32,750 | $38,350 | $43,950 | $49,550 | $55,150 | Add $5,600 for each additional |

\* "Income" means net income received, after taxes and child care costs are deducted.

The court may also waive the fees if you are currently receiving assistance under a needs-based, means-tested assistance program such as the following:
- Federal Temporary Assistance for Needy Families (TANF)
- State-provided general assistance for unemployable individuals (GA-U or GA-X)
- Federal Supplemental Security Income (SSI)
- Federal poverty-related veteran's benefits
- Food Stamp Program (FSP)

If using any of the above as the basis for waiver of filing fees, please bring evidence, such as a copy of a recent benefits award letter.

**FORMS TO USE**: The Court has standard forms for obtaining fee waivers, which you are to use even though you may have obtained similar forms elsewhere. The forms are available at no cost from the Copy Center in the Clerk's Office (2-C), the Family Law Facilitator (3-D) or online (www.courts.wa.gov/forms/?fa=forms.contribute&formID=87).

    1. Motion and Order to Waive Civil Fees and Surcharges

    2. Financial Statement (If you currently receive needs-based, means-tested benefits as identified above, you <u>do not need to complete this form</u>.)

Revised 02/2020

Superior Court Clerk's Office

**INSTRUCTIONS:**

Fill out all forms <u>completely</u>. Be sure to <u>sign</u> and <u>date</u> the Motion and Order and complete the "Financial Statement" form or obtain a copy of a recent benefits award letter.

**Delivery IN-Person**

Take the completed forms along with your completed Petition or Complaint to the *Ex Parte* Department (Room 1-J, on the 1st Floor of the Kent Regional Justice Center) to have a Commissioner review your request and sign the order.

- If the Commissioner signs the Order, you will be able to file your case without paying any fees. In a family law matter, you may be required to pay the Courthouse family law facilitator fee; also, you or your spouse may be required to pay the filing fee later if there is a joinder to the petition.
- If the waiver is denied, you will be required to pay the filing fee to file your case.

After obtaining a signed Order, take it and all your case initiating forms to the Cashier's Window in the Clerk's Office (Room 2-C, on the 2nd Floor of the Kent Regional Justice Center). <u>You must</u> file the originals of all forms the same day the Commissioner signs the order. **DO NOT remove this order from the courthouse.**

- The Ex Parte Department (Room 1-J) is open 9:00 to 11:45 a.m. and 1:30 to 4:00 p.m.
- The King County Superior Court Clerk's Office (Room 2-C) is open 9:00 am – 4:30 pm (Limited service between 12:15 – 1:15 pm).
- To contact Family Law Facilitators, call 206-477-2781.

**Delivery By MAIL**

Regional Justice Center
Attn: Clerks Office
401 Fourth Avenue North Room C2
Kent, WA 98032-4429

If you are unable to come in person or mail your Motion and Order to Waive Filing Fee and supporting documentation, please call (206) 477-0815 for assistance.

Revised 02/2020

Superior Court Clerk's Office

INSTRUCTIONS FOR
**MOTION AND ORDER TO WAIVE FILING FEES – SEATTLE LOCATION**

If you believe that you are unable to afford the civil fee and related surcharges in your civil or family law court case, you may request that the court waive it. In determining whether the filing fee should be waived, the Court will consider your ability to pay. In doing so, the court may apply a financial availability table based on 125% of the Federal Poverty Standard (see below). If there is a joint petition in a family law matter, your income will be added to your spouse's income in determining eligibility for a fee waiver.

However, the court may also waive the requirement for you to pay fees if your income is above the thresholds below, but finds that you have recurring basic living expenses which render you unable to pay the fees, or it may waive the fees if it finds there are other compelling circumstances to do so. If you are represented by a Qualified Legal Services Provider, that provider may obtain a fee waiver by presentation of the forms designated for their use.

| Family Size | 1 | 2 | 3 | 4 | 5 | 6 | 7 | 8 | 9 or more |
|---|---|---|---|---|---|---|---|---|---|
| Maximum Monthly Income* | $1,329 | $1,796 | $2,263 | $2,729 | $3,196 | $3,663 | $4,129 | $4,596 | Add $467 for each additiona |
| Maximum Annual Income* | $15,950 | $21,550 | $27,150 | $32,750 | $38,350 | $43,950 | $49,550 | $55,150 | Add $5,600 for each additional |

* "Income" means net income received, after taxes and child care costs are deducted.

The court may also waive the fees if you are currently receiving assistance under a needs-based, means-tested assistance program such as the following:
- Federal Temporary Assistance for Needy Families (TANF)
- State-provided general assistance for unemployable individuals (GA-U or GA-X)
- Federal Supplemental Security Income (SSI)
- Federal poverty-related veteran's benefits
- Food Stamp Program (FSP)

If using any of the above as the basis for waiver of fees, please bring evidence, such as a copy of a recent benefits award letter.

**FORMS TO USE**: **The Court has standard forms for obtaining fee waivers, which you are to use even though you may have obtained similar forms elsewhere. The forms are available at no cost from the Copy Center in the Clerk's Office (E609), the Family Law Facilitator (W382) or online (www.courts.wa.gov/forms/?fa=forms.contribute&formID=87).**

1. Motion and Order to Waive Civil Fees and Surcharges

2. Financial Statement (If you currently receive needs-based, means-tested benefits as identified above, you do not need to complete this form.)

Revised 02/2020

### King County
Superior Court Clerk's Office

**INSTRUCTIONS:**

Fill out all forms completely. Be sure to sign and date the Motion and Order and complete the Financial Statement" form or obtain a copy of a recent benefits award letter.

**Delivery IN-Person**

Take the completed forms along with your completed Petition or Complaint to the *Ex Parte* Department (Room W325, on the 3rd Floor of the King County Courthouse) to have a Commissioner review your request and sign the order.

- If the Commissioner signs the Order, you will be able to file your case without paying any fees. In a family law matter, you may be required to pay the Courthouse family law facilitator fee; also, you or your spouse may be required to pay the filing fee later if there is a joinder to the petition.
- If the waiver is denied, you will be required to pay the filing fee to file your case.

After obtaining a signed Order, take it and all your case initiating forms to the Cashier's Window in the Clerk's Office (Room E609, on the 6th Floor of the King County Courthouse). You must file the originals of all forms the same day the Commissioner signs the order. **DO NOT remove this order from the courthouse.**

- The Ex Parte Department (Room W325) is open 9:00 to 11:45 a.m. and 1:30 to 4:00 p.m.
- The King County Superior Court Clerk's Office (Room E609) is open 9:00 am – 4:30 pm (Limited service between 12:15 – 1:15 pm).
- To contact Family Law Facilitators, call 206-477-2553.

**Delivery By MAIL**

King County Superior Court
Attn: Clerks Office
516 Third Avenue Room E609
Seattle, WA 98104-2386

If you are unable to come in person or mail your Motion and Order to Waive Filing Fee and supporting documentation, please call (206) 477-0815 for assistance.

Revised 02/2020

## Superior Court of Washington
## County of

In re the Marriage of:

                      Petitioner,

and

                     Respondent.

No.

**Motion and Declaration for Temporary Order (MTAF)**

### I. Motion

Based on the declaration below, the undersigned moves the court for a temporary order which:

[ ]   orders temporary maintenance.
[ ]   orders child support as determined pursuant to the Washington State Support Schedule.
[ ]   approves the parenting plan which is proposed by the [ ] husband [ ] wife.
[ ]   restrains or enjoins the [ ] husband [ ] wife from transferring, removing, encumbering, concealing or in any way disposing of any property except in the usual course of business or for the necessities of life and requiring each party to notify the other of any extraordinary expenditures made after the order is issued.
[ ]   restrains or enjoins the [ ] husband [ ] wife from disturbing the peace of the other party or of any child.
[ ]   restrains or enjoins the [ ] husband [ ] wife from going onto the grounds of or entering the home, work place or school of the other party or the day care or school of the following named children: _____.
[ ]   restrains or enjoins the [ ] husband [ ] wife from knowingly coming within or knowingly remaining within _____ (distance) of the home, work place or school of the other party or the day care or school of the following children: _____.
[ ]   restrains or enjoins _____ [Name] from molesting, assaulting, harassing, or stalking _____ [Name]. (If the court orders this relief, the restrained person will be prohibited from possessing a firearm or ammunition under

# DEVELOPING A PARENTING PLAN

federal law for the duration of the order. An exception exists for law enforcement officers and military personnel when carrying department/government-issued firearms. 18 U.S.C. § 925(a)(1).)

[ ] restrains or enjoins the [ ] husband [ ] wife from removing any of the children from the state of Washington.

[ ] restrains or enjoins the [ ] husband [ ] wife from assigning, transferring, borrowing, lapsing, surrendering or changing entitlement of any insurance policies of either or both parties whether medical, health, life or auto insurance.

[ ] **(If this box is checked clear and convincing reasons for this request must be presented in the declaration below.)**
requires the [ ] husband [ ] wife to surrender any deadly weapon in his or her immediate possession or control or subject to his or her immediate possession or control to the sheriff of the county having jurisdiction of this proceeding, to his or her lawyer or to a person designated by the court.

[ ] makes each party immediately responsible for their own future debts whether incurred by credit card or loan, security interest or mortgage.

[ ] divides responsibility for the debts of the parties.

[ ] authorizes the family home to be occupied by the [ ] husband [ ] wife.

[ ] orders the use of property.

[ ] requires the [ ] husband [ ] wife to vacate the family home.

[ ] requires the [ ] husband [ ] wife to pay temporary attorney's fees, other professional fees and costs in the amount of $_____ to:

[ ] appoints a guardian ad litem on behalf of the minor children.

[ ] other:

Dated: _____    _____
                                          Signature of Moving Party or Lawyer/WSBA No.

                                          _____
                                          Print or Type Name

## II. Declaration

Temporary relief is required because:

If the surrender of deadly weapons is requested, list reasons:




[ ]   If the nonmoving party is not present and:
a) is on active duty and is a National Guard member or Reservist residing in Washington, or
b) is a dependent of a National Guard member or Reservist residing in Washington on active duty,
list the reasons why this temporary order should be granted despite the absence of the other party:




I declare under penalty of perjury under the laws of the state of Washington that the foregoing is true and correct.

Signed at _____ on _____.
                [City and State]                             [Date]

_____    _____
Signature of Moving Party                           Print or Type Name

**Do not attach financial records, personal health care records or confidential reports to this declaration. Such records should be served on the other party and filed with the court using one of these cover sheets:**

   **1) Sealed Financial Source Documents (WPF DRPSCU 09.0220) for financial records**
   **2) Sealed Personal Health Care Records (WPF DRPSCU 09.0260) for health records**
   **3) Sealed Confidential Report (WPF DRPSCU 09.270) for confidential reports**

**If filed separately using a cover sheet, the records will be sealed to protect your privacy (although they will be available to all parties in the case, their attorneys, court personnel and certain state agencies and boards.) See GR 22(C)(2).**

*Mtn/Decl for Temp Ord (MTAF) - Page 3 of 3*
*WPF DR 04.0100 (6/2006) - RCW 26.09.060; .110; .120; .194*

DEVELOPING A PARENTING PLAN 65

Case Name: _____ Case Number: _____

| Financial Statement (Attachment) |||
|---|---|---|
| 1. My name is: |||
| 2. [ ] I provide support to people who live with me:  How many?    Age(s): |||
| **3. My Monthly Income:** | **6. My Monthly Household Expenses:** ||
| Employed [ ]      Unemployed [ ] | Rent/Mortgage: | $ |
| Employer's Name: | Food/Household Supplies: | $ |
| Gross pay per month (salary or hourly pay): | $ | Utilities: | $ |
| Take home pay per month: | $ | Transportation: | $ |
| **4. Other Sources of Income Per Month in my Household:** | Ordered Maintenance actually paid: | $ |
| Source: | $ | Ordered Child Support actually paid: | $ |
| Source: | $ | Clothing: | $ |
| Source: | $ | Child Care: | $ |
| Source: | $ | Education Expenses: | $ |
| Sub-Total: | $ | Insurance (car, health): | $ |
| [ ] I receive food stamps. | Medical Expenses: | $ |
| **Total Income, lines 3 (take home pay) and 4:** | $ | Sub-Total: | $ |
| **5. My Household Assets:** | **7. My Other Monthly Household Expenses:** ||
| Cash on hand: | $ | | $ |
| Checking Account Balance: | $ | | $ |
| Savings Account Balance: | $ | | $ |
| Auto #1 (Value less loan): | $ | | $ |
| Auto #2 (Value less loan): | $ | Sub-Total: | $ |
| Home (Value less mortgage): | $ | **8. My Other Debts with Monthly Payments:** ||
| Other: | $ | | $       /mo |
| Other: | $ | | $       /mo |
| Other: | $ | | $       /mo |
| Other: | $ | | $       /mo |
| Other: | $ | Sub-Total: | $ |
| **Total Household Assets:** | $ | **Total Household Expenses and Debts, lines 6, 7, and 8:** | $ |
| Date: | Signature: ||

Financial Statement (Attachment) - Page 1 of 1
WPF GR 34.0300 (2/2011) GR 34

|                                    | No. _____ |
|---|---|
| _____ Court of Washington<br>For _____ | |
| _____<br>Petitioner/Plaintiff,<br>vs.<br>_____<br>Respondent/Defendant. | **Order Re Waiver of Civil Fees and Surcharges**<br>☐ **Granted (ORPRFP)**<br>☐ **Denied (ORDYMT)**<br>☐ Clerk's Action Required 3.1 |

## I. Basis

The court received the motion to waive fees and surcharges filed by or on behalf of the
☐ petitioner/plaintiff ☐ respondent/defendant.

## II. Findings

The Court reviewed the motion and supporting declaration(s). Based on the declaration(s) and any relevant records and files, the Court finds:

2.1 ☐ The moving party is indigent based on the following: He or she:

    ☐ is represented by a qualified legal aid provider that screened and found the applicant eligible for free civil legal aid services; and/or

    ☐ receives benefits from one or more needs-based, means-tested assistance programs; and/or

    ☐ has household income at or below 125% of the federal poverty guideline; and/or

    ☐ has household income above 125% of the federal poverty guideline but cannot meet basic household living expenses and pay the fees and/or surcharges; and/or

    ☐ other: _____
    _____
    _____.

Order re Civil Fee Waiver (ORPRFP, ORDYMT) - Page 1 of 2
WPF GR 34.0500 (05/2014) – GR 34

DEVELOPING A PARENTING PLAN

2.2 ☐ The moving party is not indigent.

2.3 ☐ Other: _____
_____
_____
_____
_____
_____

## III. Order

Based on the findings the court orders:

3.1 ☐ The motion is granted, and

    ☐ all fees and surcharges the payment of which is a condition precedent to the moving party's ability to secure access to judicial relief are waived.

    ☐ other: _____
_____
_____
_____
_____
_____

3.2 ☐ The motion is denied.

Dated: _____    _____
                                                                           **Judge/Commissioner**

Presented by:

_____
Signature of Party or Lawyer/WSBA No.

_____
Print or Type Name         Date

**Confidential Information** (CIF)

Clerk: Do **not** file in a public access file

Superior Court of Washington,
County: _____
Case No.: _____

**Important!** Only court staff and some state agencies may see this form. The other party and their lawyer may **not** see this form unless a court order allows it. State agencies may disclose the information in this form according to their *own rules*.

1. Who is completing this form? *(Name):* __John Doe_____

2. Is there a current restraining or protection order involving the parties or children? [ ] Yes [X] No
   If yes, who does the order protect? *(Name/s):* _____

3. Does your address information need to be confidential to protect your or your children's health, safety, or liberty? *(Check one):* [ ] Yes [X] No
   If yes, explain why? _____

4. **Your Information** - This person is a *(check one):* [ ] Petitioner [ ] Respondent
   Interpreter needed? [ ] Yes [ ] No   Language, if yes:_____

| Full name *(first, middle, last)*: John J Doe | Date of birth *(MM/DD/YYYY)*: 01/01/1977 | Sex: M |
|---|---|---|
| Driver's license/Identicard *(No., state)*: 12345678 | Race: BLK | Relationship to children in this case: Father |
| Mailing address *(This address will **not** be kept private.)* (street address or P.O. box, city, state zip): 777 Lane St. Somewhere, WA 99999 | | |

*If your case is **only** about a protection order, skip to section **5**.*

| Home address *(check one)*: [X] same as mailing address [ ] listed below *(street, city, state, zip)*: | | |
|---|---|---|
| Phone: (253) 555-1212 | Email: | Social Sec. No: 080-00-0000 |
| Employer's name: | | Employer's phone: |
| Employer's address: | | |

5. **Other Party's Information** – This person is a *(check one):* [ ] Petitioner [X] Respondent
   Interpreter needed? [ ] Yes [ ] No   Language, if yes: _____

| Full name *(first, middle, last)*: Jane S Doe | Date of birth *(MM/DD/YYYY)*: 02/22/1977 | Sex: F |
|---|---|---|
| Driver's license/Identicard *(No., state)*: 12347890 | Race: BLK | Relationship to children in this case: Mother |
| Mailing address *(This address will **not** be kept private.)* (street address or PO box, city, state zip): 123 Main St. Seattle, WA | | |

*If your case is **only** about a protection order, skip to section **6**.*

# DEVELOPING A PARENTING PLAN

| Home address *(check one):* [ ] same as mailing address [ ] listed below *(street, city, state, zip):* |||
|---|---|---|
| Phone: (206) 555-1111 | Email: | Social Sec. No: 000-00-0000 |
| Employer's name: || Employer's phone: |
| Employer's address: |||

> **Skip sections 6–9 if your case does not involve children. Sign at the end.**

**6. Children's Information** *(You do not have to fill out the children's Social Security numbers if your case is only about a protection order.)*

| | Child's full name *(first, middle, last)* | Date of birth *(MM/DD/YYYY)* | Race | Sex | Soc. Sec. No. | Current location: lives with |
|---|---|---|---|---|---|---|
| 1. | Jay Doe | 12/12/2010 | BLK | M | | [ ] You<br>[X] other party: _____ |
| 2. | | | | | | [ ] You<br>[ ] other party: _____ |
| 3. | | | | | | [ ] You<br>[ ] other party: _____ |
| 4. | | | | | | [ ] You<br>[ ] other party: _____ |

**7. Have the children lived with anyone other than you or the other party during the last five years?** *(Check one):* [X] No [ ] Yes   If **yes**, fill out below:

| | Children lived with *(name)* | That person's **current** address |
|---|---|---|
| 1. | | |
| 2. | | |

**8. Do other people (not parents) have custody or visitation rights to the children?**
*(Check one):* [X] No [ ] Yes   If **yes**, fill out below:

| | Person with rights *(name)* | That person's **current** address |
|---|---|---|
| 1. | | |
| 2. | | |

**9. If you are asking for custody and are not the parent, list all other adults living in your home:**

| 1. *(Name):* | Date of birth *(MM/DD/YYYY):* |
|---|---|
| 2. *(Name):* | Date of birth *(MM/DD/YYYY):* |

I declare under penalty of perjury under Washington State law that the information on this form about me is true. The information about the other party is the best information I have or is unavailable because *(explain):* _____

[ ] Check here if you need more space to list other Petitioners, Respondents, or children. Put that information on the *Attachment to Confidential Information,* form FL All Family 002, and attach it to this form.

Signed at *(city and state):* Somewhere, WA    Date: 9/27/19

▶ *John Doe*           *John Doe*
Petitioner/Respondent signs here    Print name here

RCW 26.23.050, 26.50.160, 26.27.281; GR 22
Mandatory Form *(06/2020)*
FL All Family 001

Confidential Information

**Superior Court of Washington, County of** _____

In re parenting and support of:

Children:

_Jay Doe_

Petitioner *(person who started this case)*:

_John Doe_

And Respondent *(other parent)*:

_Jane Doe_

No. _____

Summons: Notice about Petition for Parenting Plan, Residential Schedule and/or Child Support
(SM)

# Summons: Notice about Petition for Parenting Plan, Residential Schedule and/or Child Support

**To the Respondent:** The Petitioner started a case asking for a parenting and/or support order for the children listed above. You <u>must</u> respond in writing for the court to consider your side.

**Deadline!** Your *Response* must be served on the Petitioner within **20 days** of the date you were served this *Summons* (60 days if you were served outside of Washington State). If the case has been filed, you must also file your *Response* by the same deadline. If you do not serve and file your *Response* or a *Notice of Appearance* by the deadline:

- No one has to notify you about other hearings in this case, and
- The court may approve the Petitioner's requests without hearing your side (called a *default judgment*).

Follow these steps:

**1.** **Read** the *Petition* and any other documents you receive with this *Summons*. These documents explain what the Petitioner is asking for.

**2.** **Fill out** the *Response to Petition for Parenting Plan, Residential Schedule and/or Child Support* (form FL Parentage 332). You can get the *Response* and other forms at:

- Washington State Court Forms: *www.courts.wa.gov/forms,*
- Administrative Office of the Courts – call: (360) 705-5328,

- Washington LawHelp: *www.washingtonlawhelp.org*,
- Washington State Law Library: *www.courts.wa.gov/library*, or
- Superior Court Clerk's office or county law library (for a fee).

3. **Serve** (give) a copy of your *Response* to the Petitioner at the address below and to any other Respondents. You may use certified mail with return receipt requested. For more information on how to serve, read Superior Court Civil Rule 5.

4. **File** your original *Response* with the court clerk at this address:

Superior Court Clerk, _____ County

| address | city | state | zip |

**If there is no "Case No." listed on page 1,** this case may not have been filed and you will not be able to file a *Response*. Contact the Superior Court Clerk or check www.courts.wa.gov to find out.

If the case was **not** filed, you must still serve your *Response*, and you may demand that the Petitioner file this case with the court. Your demand must be in writing and must be served on the Petitioner or his/her lawyer (whoever signed this *Summons*). If the Petitioner does not file papers for this case within 14 days of being served with your demand, this service on you of the *Summons* and *Petition* will not be valid. If the Petitioner does file, then you must file your original *Response* with the court clerk at the address above.

5. **Lawyer not required:** It's a good idea to talk to a lawyer, but you may file and serve your *Response* without one.

**Petitioner or his/her lawyer fills out below:**

▶ *John Doe*        9/27/19
Signature of Petitioner **or** Lawyer     Date

John Doe
Print name (and WSBA No., if Lawyer)

I agree to accept legal papers for this case at *(check one):*

☐ my lawyer's address:

| Lawyer's address | city | state | zip |

Email *(if applicable):* _____

☒ the following address *(this does **not** have to be your home address):*

777        Somewhere     WA    99999
address        city        state    zip

Note: You and the other party/ies may agree to accept legal papers by email under Civil Rule 5 and local court rules.

*(If this address changes before the case ends, you **must** notify all parties and the court clerk in writing. You may use the Notice of Address Change form (FL All Family 120). You must also update your Confidential Information Form (FL All Family 001) if this case involves parentage or child support.)*

This Summons is issued according to Rule 4.1 of the Superior Court Civil Rules of the State of Washington.

**Superior Court of Washington, County of** _____

In re parenting and support of:

Children:
_Jay Doe_

Petitioner *(person who started this case)*:
_John Doe_

And **Respondent** *(other parent)*:
_Jane Doe_

No. _____

Petition for a Parenting Plan, Residential Schedule and/or Child Support (PTPPCS)

# Petition for a Parenting Plan, Residential Schedule and/or Child Support

*Use this form* to ask for a Parenting Plan, Residential Schedule or Child Support Order *only if* parentage has already been established by:
- *Acknowledgment of Parentage, or*
- *Court order that decided parentage.*

If parentage was established by a court order, use this form **only if** your proposed plan or schedule would not change the custodian named *in the order establishing parentage.*

1. **My name is:** _John Doe_ . **I ask the court to approve a** *(check all that apply):*

   [X] Parenting Plan or Residential Schedule   [ ] Child Support Order.

2. **Children**

   Respondent *(name):* _Jane Doe_ , and I are parents of the following children:

   | | Child's name | Age | Lives with: | In (county and state): |
   |---|---|---|---|---|
   | 1. | Jay Doe | 9 | [ ] Petitioner | King WA |

RCW 26.26B.020(7)(b)
Mandatory Form *(03/2020)*
FL Parentage 331

Petition for a Parenting Plan, Res. Sched. and/or Child Support

## DEVELOPING A PARENTING PLAN

|   | Child's name | Age | Lives with: | In (county and state): |
|---|---|---|---|---|
|   |   |   | [x] Respondent |   |
| 2. |   |   | [ ] Petitioner<br>[ ] Respondent |   |
| 3. |   |   | [ ] Petitioner<br>[ ] Respondent |   |
| 4. |   |   | [ ] Petitioner<br>[ ] Respondent |   |
| 5. |   |   | [ ] Petitioner<br>[ ] Respondent |   |

3. **Was parentage established by court order?**

   *(Repeat this section for each child as needed.)*

   [x] **No**. Parentage was established by *Acknowledgment of Parentage*. *(Skip to 4.)*

   [ ] **Yes**. A court signed a *Final Parentage Order* or other order establishing parentage for *(child's name):* _____, but the court did not sign a *Parenting Plan* or *Residential Schedule* for that child.

   The parentage order was signed in *(county/state):* _____,
   in case number: _____ on *(date):* _____.
   ➤ Attach or file a certified copy of the parentage order **if** it was issued in a different county or state from where you are filing this Petition.

   The parentage order named *(parent):* _____
   as custodian. My proposed plan or schedule would **not** change the custodian named in the parentage order.
   ➤ If you want to change the custodian, you must file a Petition to Change a Parenting Plan, Residential Schedule or Custody Order (form FL Modify 601) instead of this Petition.

4. **Was parentage established by Acknowledgment of Parentage?**

   *(Repeat this section for each child as needed.)*

   [ ] **No**. Parentage was established by court order as described above. *(Skip to 5.)*

   [x] **Yes**. The Petitioner and Respondent signed an *Acknowledgment of Parentage* for *(child's name):* __Jay Doe_____ that was filed with the appropriate agency of the State of ____WA_____ on *(date):* 12/12/2010.
   ➤ You must file a copy of the Birth Certificate or Acknowledgment of Parentage with this petition. Use a cover sheet (form FL Parentage 329) to keep it private (sealed).

   Was the mother married or in a registered domestic partnership when the child was born (or within 300 days before)?

   [x] **No**. *(Skip to 5.)*

[ ] **Yes**. Her spouse/partner *(name)* _____,
signed a *Denial of Parentage* that was filed with the appropriate agency of the
State of _____ on *(date)* _____.
> You must file a copy of the Denial of Parentage with this petition. Use a cover sheet (form FL Parentage 329) to keep it private (sealed).

**5. Was an Acknowledgment of Parentage filed in Washington State?**

*(Repeat this section for each child as needed.)*

[ ] **No**. Parentage was established by court order as described above. *(Skip to 6.)*

[ ] **No**. Parentage was established by *Acknowledgment of Parentage* in a different state than Washington. *(Skip to 6.)*

[X] **Yes**. The *Acknowledgment of Parentage* for *(child's name):* ___Jay Doe___ was filed in Washington State.

   a. **Effective date** – The *Acknowledgment of Parentage* (and *Denial*, if any) became effective (valid) on the date the child was born or the date the *Acknowledgment of Parentage* (and *Denial*, if any) was filed with the Washington State Registrar of Vital Statistics, whichever was later.

   b. **Deadline to withdraw** – The deadline to withdraw (rescind) the *Acknowledgment of Parentage* or *Denial* has passed because:

      [ ] it has been **more** than 60 days from the effective date.

      [ ] it has been **less** than 60 days from the effective date; **but** everyone who signed the *Acknowledgment* (and *Denial*, if any) was before the court to decide an issue about the child on *(date)* _____.

   c. **Deadline to challenge** – *(check one):*

      [ ] The deadline to challenge the *Acknowledgment of Parentage* or *Denial* has passed. It has been **more** than four years since the effective date.

      [ ] The deadline to challenge the *Acknowledgment of Parentage* or *Denial* has **not** passed. It has been **less** than four years since the effective date; **but** the Petitioner says:
      - The child's acknowledged father is the father,
      - No court has said that another man is the child's father,
      - There are no other open court cases to decide who the child's father is, **and**
      - Notice has been given to all other men who claimed to be this child's father.

**6. Jurisdiction over parents**

*Fill out below to say if a Washington state court has personal jurisdiction (authority to make decisions) over the Respondent (name):* _____.

**Basis for personal jurisdiction** *(check all that apply):*

[X] Will be served in Washington

[x] Lives in Washington now
[ ] Lived in Washington with child
[ ] Lived in Washington and paid pregnancy costs or support for child
[ ] Caused child to live in Washington
[ ] Had sex in Washington that may have produced the child
[ ] Signed a Washington Acknowledgment of Parentage
[ ] Had parentage established by a Washington state court order
[ ] Agrees to Washington deciding
[ ] None of the above (no personal jurisdiction)

> **Warning!** If the court does **not** have personal jurisdiction over the Respondent, it cannot order child support, fees costs, or restraining orders.

7.  **Children's Home/s**

    During the past 5 years have any of the children lived:
    - on an Indian reservation,
    - outside Washington state,
    - in a foreign country, or
    - with anyone who is not a party to this case?

    [x] No. *(Skip to 8.)*

    [ ] Yes. *(Fill out below to show where each child has lived during the last 5 years.)*

| Dates | Children | Lived with | In which state, Indian reservation, or foreign country |
|---|---|---|---|
| From: <br> To: | [ ] All children <br> [ ] *(Name/s):* | [ ] Petitioner [ ] Respondent <br> [ ] Other *(name):* | |
| From: <br> To: | [ ] All children <br> [ ] *(Name/s):* | [ ] Petitioner [ ] Respondent <br> [ ] Other *(name):* | |
| From: <br> To: | [ ] All children <br> [ ] *(Name/s):* | [ ] Petitioner [ ] Respondent <br> [ ] Other *(name):* | |
| From: <br> To: | [ ] All children <br> [ ] *(Name/s):* | [ ] Petitioner [ ] Respondent <br> [ ] Other *(name):* | |
| From: <br> To: | [ ] All children <br> [ ] *(Name/s):* | [ ] Petitioner [ ] Respondent <br> [ ] Other *(name):* | |

8. **Other people with a legal right to spend time with a child**

    Do you know of anyone besides the Petitioner and Respondent who has or claims to have a legal right to spend time with any of the children?

    *(Check one):* [X] No. *(Skip to **9**.)* [ ] Yes. *(Fill out below.)*

    | Name of person | Children this person may have the right to spend time with |
    |---|---|
    | | [ ] All children<br>[ ] *(Name/s):* |
    | | [ ] All children<br>[ ] *(Name/s):* |

9. **Other court cases involving a child**

    Do you know of any court cases involving any of the children?

    *(Check one):* [X] No. *(Skip to **10**.)* [ ] Yes. *(Fill out below.)*

    | Kind of case<br>(Family Law, Criminal, Protection Order, Juvenile, Dependency, Other) | County and State | Case number and year | Children |
    |---|---|---|---|
    | | | | [ ] All children<br>[ ] *(Name/s):* |
    | | | | [ ] All children<br>[ ] *(Name/s):* |
    | | | | [ ] All children<br>[ ] *(Name/s):* |
    | | | | [ ] All children<br>[ ] *(Name/s):* |

10. **Jurisdiction over children** (RCW 26.27.201 – .221, .231, .261, .271)

    The court can order a *Parenting Plan* or *Residential Schedule* for the children because *(check all that apply; if a box applies to all of the children, you may write "the children" instead of listing names):*

    [ ] **Exclusive, continuing jurisdiction** – A Washington court has already made a custody order or parenting plan for the children, and the court still has authority to make other orders for *(children's names):* _____.

    [X] **Home state jurisdiction** – Washington is the children's home state because *(check all that apply):*

[X] *(Children's names):* _____Jay Doe_____ lived in Washington with a parent or someone acting **as a parent** for at least the 6 months just before this case was filed, or if the children are less than 6 months old, they have lived in Washington with a parent or someone acting as a parent since birth.

  [ ] There were times the children were not in Washington in the 6 months just before this case was filed (or since birth if they are less than 6 months old), but those were temporary absences.

[ ] *(Children's names):* _____
do not live in Washington right now, but Washington was the children's home state sometime in the 6 months just before this case was filed, and a parent or someone acting as a parent of the children still lives in Washington.

[ ] *(Children's names):* _____
do not have another home state.

[X] **No home state or home state declined** – No court of any other state (or tribe) has the jurisdiction to make decisions for *(children's names):* _____Jay Doe_____, **or** a court in the children's home state (or tribe) decided it is better to have this case in Washington **and:**

  - The children and a parent or someone acting as a parent have ties to Washington beyond just living here; **and**
  - There is a lot of information (substantial evidence) about the children's care, protection, education, and relationships in this state.

[ ] **Other state declined** – The courts in other states (or tribes) that might be *(children's names):* _____'s home state have refused to take this case because it is better to have this case in Washington.

[ ] **Temporary emergency jurisdiction** – The court can make decisions for *(children's names):* _____ because the children are in this state now **and** were abandoned here **or** need emergency protection because the children (or the children's parent, brother, or sister) were abused or threatened with abuse. *(Check one):*

  [ ] A custody case involving the children was filed in the children's home state *(name of state or tribe):* _____. Washington should take temporary emergency jurisdiction over the children until the Petitioner can get a court order from the children's home state (or tribe).

  [ ] There is **no** valid custody order or open custody case in the children's home state *(name of state or tribe):* _____. If no case is filed *in the children's home state (or tribe)* by the time the children have been in Washington for 6 months, *(date):* _____, Washington should have final jurisdiction over the children.

[ ] Other reason *(specify):* _____

_____

## 11. Parenting Plan or Residential Schedule

Has a court already approved a *Parenting Plan* or *Residential Schedule*?

*Check one:* [ ] Yes [X] No

➢ If **Yes:**

My plan or schedule was approved by a court on *(date)*: _____

in *(county/state)*: _____

in case number: _____.

➢ If **No:** Do you want the court to order a *Parenting Plan* or *Residential Schedule*?

*Check one:* [x] Yes [ ] No

If *Yes:* My proposed *Parenting Plan* (form FL All Family 140) or *Residential Schedule* (form FL Parentage 303) *(check one):* [ ] is attached [ ] will be filed and served at a later date.

> *Important!* The court can order a *Parenting Plan* or *Residential Schedule* in this case only if a court has not already approved one. To change an earlier plan or schedule, use the *Petition to Change a Parenting Plan, Residential Schedule or Custody Order* (form FL Modify 601).

## 12. Child Support

[ ] There is no need for the court to make a child support order because a child support order has already been established.

My child support order was approved on *(date)*: _____

by a [ ] court [ ] agency in *(county/state)*: _____

In case number: _____.

[ ] I ask the court to order child support. (Check the orders you want the court to approve):

    [ ] Order child support, including medical support, according to state law.

    [ ] Order the Respondent to pay past support, medical costs, and other costs for the children.

[ ] The court does not have jurisdiction to order child support.

> *Important!* The court can approve a child support order in this case only if a court has not already approved one. To change an earlier child support order that was approved by a court, use the *Petition to Modify Child Support Order* (form FL Modify 501) or *Motion to Adjust Child Support Order* (form FL Modify 521).
>
> You **can** get a new child support order in this case if your earlier order was from an agency such as the Division of Child Support (DCS).

## 13. Protection Order

*Do you want the court to issue an Order for Protection as part of the final orders in this case?*

[x] **No.** I do not want an *Order for Protection*

[ ] **Yes.** *(You must file a Petition for Order for Protection, form DV-1.015 for domestic violence, or form UHST-02.0200 for harassment. You may file your Petition for Order for Protection using the same case number assigned to this case.)*

> *Important!* If you need protection **now**, ask the court clerk about getting a *Temporary Order for Protection*.

[ ] **There already is an *Order for Protection* between the other parent and me.**
*(Attach a copy of the Order for Protection if you have one):*

Court that issued the order: _____

Case number: _____

Expiration date: _____

[ ] The court does not have jurisdiction to enter a protection order.

## 14. Restraining Order

*Do you want the court to issue a Restraining Order as part of the final orders in this case?*

[X] **No.** *(Skip to 15.)*

[ ] **Yes.** *Check the type of orders you want:*

- [ ] **Do not disturb** – Order the Respondent not to disturb my peace or the peace of any child listed in **2**.

- [ ] **Stay away** – Order the Respondent not to go onto the grounds of or enter my home, workplace, or school, and the daycare or school of any child listed in **2**.
    - [ ] Also, not knowingly to go or stay within _____ feet of my home, workplace, or school, or the daycare or school of any child listed in **2**.

- [ ] **Do not hurt or threaten** – Order the Respondent:
    - Not to assault, harass, stalk or molest me or any child listed in **2**; and
    - Not to use, try to use, or threaten to use physical force against me or the children that would reasonably be expected to cause bodily injury.

    > *Warning!* If the court makes this order, the court must consider if weapons restrictions are required by state law; federal law may also prohibit the Restrained Person from possessing firearms or ammunition.

- [ ] **Prohibit weapons and order surrender** – Order the Respondent:
    - Not to access, possess, or obtain any firearms, other dangerous weapons, or concealed pistol licenses until the Order ends, and
    - To immediately surrender any firearms, other dangerous weapons, and any concealed pistol licenses that he/she possesses to *(check one):* [ ] the police chief or sheriff. [ ] his/her lawyer. [ ] other person *(name):* _____.

[ ] **Other orders:** _____

> *Important!* If you want a restraining order *now*, you must file a Motion for Temporary Family Law Order and Restraining Order (FL Parentage 323) or a Motion for Immediate Restraining Order (Ex Parte) (FL Parentage 321).

## 15. Fees and Costs

[X] Does not apply.

[ ] I ask the court to order the Respondent to pay lawyer fees, guardian ad litem fees, court costs, and other reasonable costs.

## 16. Other Orders

[X] Does not apply.

[ ] I ask the court to order *(specify):* _____

_____

## 17. Summary of Requests

I ask the court to approve the following orders *(check all that apply):*

[X] Petitioner's proposed *Parenting Plan* or *Residential Schedule*

[ ] *Child Support Order,* according to the Washington State Child Support Schedule

[ ] *Order for Protection*

[ ] *Restraining Order*

[ ] Payment of lawyer fees, guardian ad litem fees, court costs, and other reasonable costs.

[ ] Other *(specify):* _____

_____

**Petitioner fills out below:**

I declare under penalty of perjury under the laws of the state of Washington that the facts I have provided on this form are true.

Signed at *(city and state):* ___Somewhere WA___  Date: __9/27/19__

▶ ___John Doe___                    ___John Doe___
Petitioner signs here                Print name

**Petitioner's lawyer (if any) fills out below:**

▶ _____  _____  _____
Petitioner's lawyer signs here    Print name and WSBA No.        Date

[ ] **Respondent fills out below if s/he agrees to join this Petition:**

I, *(name):* _____, agree to join this *Petition.* I understand that if I fill out and sign below, the court may approve the requests listed in this *Petition* unless I file and serve a *Response* before the court signs final orders. *(Check one):*

[ ] I do not need to be notified about the court's hearings or decisions in this case.

[ ] I ask the Petitioner to notify me about any hearings in this case. *(List an address where you agree to accept legal documents. This may be a lawyer's address or any other address.)*

_____
address                            city               state        zip

*(If this address changes before the case ends, you **must** notify all parties and the court clerk in writing. You may use the Notice of Address Change form (FL All Family 120). You must also update your Confidential Information Form (FL All Family 001) if this case involves parentage or child support.)*

▶ _____  _____  _____
Respondent signs here              Print name                    Date

RCW 26.26B.020(7)(b)          Petition for a Parenting Plan, Res.
Mandatory Form *(03/2020)*    Sched. and/or Child Support
FL Parentage 331

**Superior Court of Washington, County of** _____

In re:

Petitioner/s *(person/s who started this case)*:

___John Doe___

And Respondent/s *(other party/parties)*:

___Jane Doe___

No. _____

Sealed Birth Certificate or Parentage Document (Cover Sheet)
(XSADP)
☒ Clerk's action required

# Sealed Birth Certificate or Parentage Document
## (Cover Sheet)

Use this form as a cover sheet to keep your documents **private** from the public. On the first page of each document, write the word "SEALED" 1 inch from the top of the page.

Check the documents you are attaching to this cover sheet to be sealed:

☒ Birth Certificate

☐ Acknowledgment of Parentage

☐ Denial of Parentage

Submitted by: ☒ Petitioner or his/her lawyer ☐ Respondent or his/her lawyer

▶ ___John Doe___  ___John Doe___
Sign here  *Print name (and WSBA No., if lawyer )*

**Important!** The other person and the lawyers in your case can see your **sealed** documents. If you need to keep your address information private for safety reasons, you may cross out or delete your address information.

GR 22(d)(2)
Optional Form *(01/2019)*
**FL Parentage 329**

**Superior Court of Washington, County of** _____

In re:

Petitioner/s *(person/s who started this case)*:
_____*John Doe*_____

And Respondent/s *(other party/parties)*:
_____*Jane Doe*_____

No. _____

Parenting Plan
(PPP / PPT / PP)

Clerk's action required: **1**

# Parenting Plan

**1.** This parenting plan is a *(check one)*:

[ ] **Proposal** (request) by a parent *(name/s)*: _____*John Doe*_____.
It is not a signed court order. (PPP)

[ ] **Court order** signed by a judge or commissioner. This is a *(check one)*:

[ ] Temporary order. (PPT)
[ ] Final order. (PP)
[ ] This final parenting plan changes the last final parenting plan.

**2. Children** – This parenting plan is for the following children:

| | Child's name | Age | | Child's name | Age |
|---|---|---|---|---|---|
| 1. | Jay Doe | 9 | 4. | | |
| 2. | | | 5. | | |
| 3. | | | 6. | | |

**3. Reasons for putting limitations on a parent** (under RCW 26.09.191)

**a. Abandonment, neglect, child abuse, domestic violence, assault, or sex offense.**
*(If a parent has any of these problems, the court **must** limit that parent's contact with the children and that parent's right to make decisions for the children, and may not require dispute resolution other than court.)*

[X] Neither parent has any of these problems. (*Skip to **3.b.***)

[ ] A parent has one or more of these problems as follows *(check all that apply):*

- [ ] **Abandonment** – *(Parent's name):* _____
  intentionally abandoned a child listed in **2** for an extended time.

- [ ] **Neglect** – *(Parent's name):* _____
  substantially refused to perform his/her parenting duties for a child listed in **2**.

- [ ] **Child Abuse** – *(Parent's name):* _____
  (or someone living in that parent's home) abused or threatened to abuse a child. The abuse was *(check all that apply):*
  [ ] physical   [ ] sexual   [ ] repeated emotional abuse.

- [ ] **Domestic Violence** – *(Parent's name):* _____
  (or someone living in that parent's home) has a history of domestic violence as defined in RCW 26.50.010.

- [ ] **Assault** – *(Parent's name):* _____
  (or someone living in that parent's home) has assaulted or sexually assaulted someone causing grievous physical harm, causing fear of such harm, or resulting in a pregnancy.

- [ ] **Sex Offense** –
  - [ ] *(Parent's name):* _____
    has been convicted of a sex offense as an adult.
  - [ ] Someone living in *(parent's name):* _____'s home has been convicted as an adult or adjudicated as a juvenile of a sex offense.

b. **Other problems** that may harm the children's best interests. *(If a parent has any of these problems, the court **may** limit that parent's contact with the children and that parent's right to make decisions for the children.)*

[ ] Neither parent has any of these problems. (*Skip to **4.***)

[ ] A parent has one or more of these problems as follows *(check all that apply):*

- [ ] **Neglect** – *(Parent's name):* _____
  neglected his/her parental duties towards a child listed in **2**.

- [ ] **Emotional or physical problem** – *(Parent's name):* _____
  _____ has a long-term emotional or physical problem that gets in the way of his/her ability to parent.

- [ ] **Substance Abuse** – *(Parent's name):* _____
  has a long-term problem with drugs, alcohol, or other substances that gets in the way of his/her ability to parent.

- [ ] **Lack of emotional ties** – *(Parent's name):* _____
  has few or no emotional ties with a child listed in **2**.

- [ ] **Abusive use of conflict** – *(Parent's name):* _____
  uses conflict in a way that may cause serious damage to the psychological development of a child listed in **2**.

- [X] **Withholding the child** – *(Parent's name):* ____*Jane Doe*____
  has kept the other parent away from a child listed in **2** for a long time, without a

good reason.

[ ] **Other** *(specify)*: _____

4. **Limitations on a parent**

[ ] Does not apply. There are no reasons for limitations checked in **3.a.** or **3.b.** above. *(Skip to **5**.)*

[ ] **No limitations despite reasons** *(explain why there are no limitations on a parent even though there are reasons for limitations checked in **3.a.** or **3.b.** above)*: _____
_____

[ ] **The following limits or conditions apply to** *(parent's name)*: _____
_____ *(check all that apply)*:

    [ ] No contact with the children.

    [ ] Limited contact as shown in the Parenting Time Schedule (sections **8 – 11**) below.

    [ ] Limited contact as follows *(specify schedule, list all contact **here** instead of in the Parenting Time Schedule)*: _____
_____
_____

    [ ] **Supervised contact.** All parenting time shall be supervised. Any costs of supervision must be paid by *(name)*: _____
The supervisor shall be:

        [ ] a professional supervisor *(name)*: _____
        [ ] a non-professional supervisor *(name)*: _____

The dates and times of supervised contact will be:

        [ ] as shown in the Parenting Time Schedule (sections **8 – 11**) below.
        [ ] as follows *(specify)*: _____
_____

*(Specific rules for supervision, if any)*: _____
_____

    [ ] Other limitations or conditions during parenting time *(specify)*: _____
_____
_____

[ ] **Evaluation or treatment required.** *(Name)*: _____ must:

    [ ] be evaluated for: _____.

    [ ] start (or continue) and comply with treatment:

        [ ] as recommended by the evaluation.
        [ ] as follows *(specify kind of treatment and any other details)*: _____
_____

    [ ] provide a copy of the evaluation and compliance reports *(specify details)*: _____

DEVELOPING A PARENTING PLAN

If this parent does not follow the evaluation or treatment requirements above, then *(what happens):* _____

## 5. Decision-making

When the children are with you, you are responsible for them. You can make day-to-day decisions for the children when they are with you, including decisions about safety and emergency health care. Major decisions must be made as follows:

### a. Who can make major decisions about the children?

| Type of Major Decision | Joint *(parents make these decisions together)* | Limited *(only the parent named below has authority to make these decisions)* |
|---|---|---|
| School / Educational | [X] | [ ] *(Name):* |
| Health care (not emergency) | [X] | [ ] *(Name):* |
| Other: | [ ] | [ ] *(Name):* |
| Other: | [ ] | [ ] *(Name):* |
| Other: | [ ] | [ ] *(Name):* |

### b. Reasons for limits on major decision-making, if any:

[X] There are no reasons to limit major decision-making.

[ ] Major decision-making **must** be limited because one of the parents has problems as described in **3.a.** above.

[ ] Major decision-making **should** be limited because *(check all that apply)*:

  [ ] Both parents are against shared decision-making.
  [ ] One of the parents does not want to share decision-making and this is reasonable because of:
    [ ] problems as described in **3.b.** above.
    [ ] the history of each parent's participation in decision-making.
    [ ] the parents' ability and desire to cooperate with each other in decision-making.
    [ ] the distance between the parents' homes makes it hard to make timely decisions together.

## 6. Dispute Resolution

*Important!* After this parenting plan is signed by a judge or commissioner, if you and the other parent disagree about shared decisions or what parts of this plan mean, the court may require you to use a dispute resolution provider before going back to court. The court may only require a dispute resolution provider if there are **no** limitations in **3.a.** above. If a dispute resolution provider is checked below, the parents may, and sometimes must, use this provider before filing a Petition to Change a Parenting Plan or a Motion for Contempt for not following the plan. Check your county's Local Court Rules.

a. The parents will go to *(check one):*

[ ] The dispute resolution provider below (before they may go to court):

    [ ] Mediation *(mediator or agency name):* _____

    [ ] Arbitration *(arbitrator or agency name):* _____

    [ ] Counseling *(counselor or agency name):* _____

If a dispute resolution provider is not named above or if the named provider is no longer available, the parents may agree on a provider or ask the court to name one.

***Important!*** Unless there is an emergency, the parents must participate in the dispute resolution process listed above in good faith, before going to court for disagreements about joint decisions or what parts of this plan mean. This section does **not** apply to disagreements about money or support.

[X] Court (without having to go to mediation, arbitration, or counseling).
*(If you check this box, skip to section **7** below and do not fill out **6.b.**)*

b. If mediation, arbitration, or counseling is required, one parent must notify the other parent by *(check one):* [ ] certified mail  [ ] other *(specify):* _____.

The parents will pay for the mediation, arbitration, or counseling services as follows *(check one):*

[ ] *(Name):* _____ will pay _____%,
    *(Name):* _____ will pay _____%.

[ ] based on each parents' Proportional Share of Income (percentage) from line 6 of the *Child Support Worksheet*.

[ ] as decided through the dispute resolution process.

**What to expect in the dispute resolution process:**
- Preference shall be given to carrying out the parenting plan.
- If you reach an agreement, it must be put into writing, signed, and both parents must get a copy.
- If the court finds that you have used or frustrated the dispute resolution process without a good reason, the court can order you to pay financial sanctions (penalties) including the other parent's legal fees.
- You may go back to court if the dispute resolution process doesn't solve the disagreement or if you disagree with the arbitrator's decision.

## 7. Custodian

The custodian is *(name):* _____Jane Doe_____ solely for the purpose of all state and federal **statutes** which require a designation or determination of custody. Even though one parent is called the custodian, this does not change the parenting rights and responsibilities described in this plan.

*(Washington law generally refers to parenting time and decision-making, rather than custody. However, some state and federal laws require that one person be named the custodian. The custodian is the person with whom the children are scheduled to reside a majority of their time.)*

DEVELOPING A PARENTING PLAN

> **Parenting Time Schedule** *(Residential Provisions)*

Check one:

[ ] **Limited schedule only** – The children live with *(name)*: _____
and have no contact with the other parent except as described in section **4**.

*(You may **skip** the parenting time schedule in sections **8 – 11**, unless you want a different Summer or Holiday schedule, including to give uninterrupted time for vacation and holidays to the parent **not** subject to limitations.)*

[ ] **Complete** the parenting time schedule in sections **8 – 11**.

**8. School Schedule**

    **a. Children under school-age**

        [X] Does not apply. All children are school-age.

        [ ] The schedule for children under school-age is the same as for school-age children.

        [ ] Children under school-age are scheduled to live with *(name)*: _____, except when they are scheduled to live with *(name)*: _____ on *(check all that apply)*:

            [ ] WEEKENDS: [ ] every week [ ] every other week [ ] other *(specify)*: _____

                from *(day)* _____ at ___:___ __.m. to *(day)* _____ at ___:___ __.m.

                from *(day)* _____ at ___:___ __.m. to *(day)* _____ at ___:___ __.m.

            [ ] WEEKDAYS: [ ] every week [ ] every other week [ ] other *(specify)*: _____

                from *(day)* _____ at ___:___ __.m. to *(day)* _____ at ___:___ __.m.

                from *(day)* _____ at ___:___ __.m. to *(day)* _____ at ___:___ __.m.

            [ ] OTHER *(specify)*: _____
_____

        [ ] Other *(specify)*: _____
_____
_____

    **b. School-age children**

        This schedule will apply *(check one)*:

        [ ] immediately.

        [ ] when the youngest child enters *(check one)*: [ ] Kindergarten [ ] 1st grade

        [ ] when the oldest child enters *(check one)*: [ ] Kindergarten [ ] 1st grade

        [X] Other: ___When each child begins 4th grade_____

        The children are scheduled to live with *(name)*: ___Jane Doe_____,
except when they are scheduled to live with *(name)*: ___John Doe_____ on *(check all that apply)*:

[X] **WEEKENDS:** [X] every week  [ ] every other week  [ ] other *(specify):* _____

   from (day) __FRI__ at __6:00__ p.m. to (day) __SUN__ at __6:00__ p.m.

   from (day) _____ at ___:___ __.m. to (day) _____ at ___:___ __.m.

[ ] **WEEKDAYS:** [ ] every week  [ ] every other week  [ ] other *(specify):* _____

   from (day) _____ at ___:___ __.m. to (day) _____ at ___:___ __.m.

   from (day) _____ at ___:___ __.m. to (day) _____ at ___:___ __.m.

[ ] OTHER *(specify):* _____
_____

[ ] Other *(specify):* _____
_____

## 9. Summer Schedule

Summer begins and ends  [ ] according to the school calendar.  [ ] as follows: _____
_____
_____.

[ ] The Summer Schedule is the **same** as the School Schedule. *(Skip to **10**.)*

[X] The Summer Schedule is the **same** as the School Schedule **except** that each parent shall spend ___3___ weeks of uninterrupted vacation time with the children each summer. The parents shall confirm their vacation schedules in writing by the end of *(date)* _____ each year. *(Skip to **10**.)*

[ ] The Summer Schedule is **different** than the School Schedule. The Summer Schedule will begin the summer before *(check one):*  [ ] the youngest child
  [ ] the oldest child
  [ ] each child

begins *(check one):*  [ ] Kindergarten  [ ] 1st grade  [ ] Other: _____

During the summer the children are scheduled to live with *(name):* _____, except when they are scheduled to live with *(name):* _____ on *(check all that apply):*

   [ ] **WEEKENDS:** [ ] every week  [ ] every other week  [ ] other *(specify):* _____

   from (day) _____ at ___:___ __.m. to (day) _____ at ___:___ __.m.

   from (day) _____ at ___:___ __.m. to (day) _____ at ___:___ __.m.

   [ ] **WEEKDAYS:** [ ] every week  [ ] every other week  [ ] other *(specify):* _____

   from (day) _____ at ___:___ __.m. to (day) _____ at ___:___ __.m.

   from (day) _____ at ___:___ __.m. to (day) _____ at ___:___ __.m.

   [ ] OTHER *(specify):* _____
   _____

DEVELOPING A PARENTING PLAN

**10. Holiday Schedule (includes school breaks and special occasions)**

[ ] The Holiday Schedule is the **same** as the School and Summer Schedules above for all holidays, school breaks, and special occasions. *(Skip to **11**.)*

[ ] The children are scheduled to spend holidays, school breaks, and special occasions as follows:
*(Check all that apply. Note any differences for children who have not yet started school.)*

[ ] **Martin Luther King Jr. Day** – Begins and ends *(day/time)*: _____
    [ ] Odd years with *(name)*: _____; Even years with the other parent
    [ ] Every year with *(name)*: _____
    [ ] With the parent who has the children for the attached weekend
    [ ] Other plan: _____

[ ] **Presidents' Day** – Begins and ends *(day/time)*: _____
    [ ] Odd years with *(name)*: _____; Even years with the other parent
    [ ] Every year with *(name)*: _____
    [ ] With the parent who has the children for the attached weekend
    [ ] Other plan: _____

[ ] **Mid-winter Break** – Begins and ends *(day/time)*: _____
    [ ] Odd years with *(name)*: _____; Even years with the other parent
    [ ] Every year with *(name)*: _____
    [ ] Each parent has the children for the half of break attached to his/her weekend. The children must be exchanged on Wednesday at (time): _____
    [ ] Other plan: _____

[ ] **Spring Break** – Begins and ends *(day/time)*: _____
    [ ] Odd years with *(name)*: _____; Even years with the other parent
    [ ] Every year with *(name)*: _____
    [ ] Each parent has the children for the half of break attached to his/her weekend. The children must be exchanged on Wednesday at (time): _____
    [ ] Other plan: _____

[ ] **Mother's Day** – Begins and ends *(day/time)*: _____
    [ ] Odd years with *(name)*: _____; Even years with the other parent
    [X] Every year with *(name)*: *Jane Doe*
    [ ] Other plan: _____

[ ] **Memorial Day** – Begins and ends *(day/time)*: _____
    [ ] Odd years with *(name)*: _____; Even years with the other parent
    [ ] Every year with *(name)*: _____
    [ ] With the parent who has the children for the attached weekend
    [ ] Other plan: _____

[ ] **Father's Day** – Begins and ends *(day/time)*: _____

[ ] Odd years with *(name)*: _____; Even years with the other parent
[X] Every year with *(name)*: _John Doe_____
[ ] Other plan: _____

[ ] **Fourth of July** – Begins and ends *(day/time)*: _____
    [X] Odd years with *(name)*: _____; Even years with the other parent
    [ ] Every year with *(name)*: _____
    [ ] Follow the Summer Schedule in section **9.**
    [ ] Other plan: _____

[ ] **Labor Day** – Begins and ends *(day/time)*: _____
    [ ] Odd years with *(name)*: _____; Even years with the other parent
    [ ] Every year with *(name)*: _____
    [ ] With the parent who has the children for the attached weekend
    [ ] Other plan: _____

[ ] **Thanksgiving Day / Break** – Begins and ends *(day/time)*: _____
    [X] Odd years with *(name)*: _Jane Doe_____; Even years with the other parent
    [ ] Every year with *(name)*: _____
    [ ] Other plan: _____
    _____
    _____

[ ] **Winter Break** – Begins and ends *(day/time)*: _____
    [ ] Odd years with *(name)*: _____; Even years with the other parent
    [ ] Every year with *(name)*: _____
    [ ] Other plan: _____
    _____
    _____

[ ] **Christmas Eve / Day** – Begins and ends *(day/time)*: _____
    [X] Odd years with *(name)*: _Jane Doe_____; Even years with the other parent
    [ ] Every year with *(name)*: _____
    [ ] Follow the Winter Break schedule above.
    [ ] Other plan: _____
    _____
    _____

[ ] **New Year's Eve / Day** – Begins and ends *(day/time)*: _____
    *(odd/even is based on New Year's Eve)*
    [X] Odd years with *(name)*: _Jane Doe_____; Even years with the other parent
    [ ] Every year with *(name)*: _____

[ ] Follow the Winter Break schedule above.
[ ] Other plan: _____

[ ] **All three-day weekends not listed elsewhere**
*(Federal holidays, school in-service days, etc.)*
[ ] The children shall spend any unspecified holiday or non-school day with the parent who has them for the attached weekend.
[ ] Other plan: _____

> *Important!* Families in Washington observe a broad range of religions and traditions. Your Parenting Plan can provide for how children will spend time on other significant days. (Examples: Eid, Passover, Easter, Chinese New Year, birthdays, etc.) Add lines as needed.

[ ] **Other occasion important to the family:** _Children's birthdays_
   Begins and ends *(day/time)*: _____
   [X] Odd years with *(name)*: _Jane Doe_ ; Even years with the other parent
   [ ] Every year with *(name)*: _____
   [ ] Other plan: _____

[ ] **Other occasion important to the family:** _____
   Begins and ends *(day/time)*: _____
   [ ] Odd years with *(name)*: _____; Even years with the other parent
   [ ] Every year with *(name)*: _____
   [ ] Other plan: _____

[ ] **Other occasion important to the family:** _____
   Begins and ends *(day/time)*: _____
   [ ] Odd years with *(name)*: _____; Even years with the other parent
   [ ] Every year with *(name)*: _____
   [ ] Other plan: _____

## 11. Conflicts in Scheduling

The Holiday Schedule must be observed over all other schedules. If there are conflicts within the Holiday Schedule *(check all that apply)*:

[ ] Named holidays shall be followed before school breaks.

[X] Children's birthdays shall be followed before named holidays and school breaks.

[ ] Other *(specify)*: _____
_____
_____

## 12. Transportation Arrangements

The children will be exchanged for parenting time (picked up and dropped off) at:
- [X] each parent's home
- [ ] school or daycare, when in session
- [ ] other location *(specify)*: _____

_____

Who is responsible for arranging transportation?
- [X] The **picking up** parent – The parent who is about to **start** parenting time with the children must arrange to have the children picked up.
- [X] The **dropping off** parent – The parent whose parenting time is **ending** must arrange to have the children dropped off.

Other details (if any): _____

_____
_____
_____

## 13. Moving with the Children (Relocation)

Anyone with majority or substantially equal residential time (at least 45 percent) who wants to move with the children **must notify** every other person who has court-ordered time with the children.

### *Move to a different school district*

If the move is to a different school district, the relocating person must complete the form *Notice of Intent to Move with Children* (FL Relocate 701) and deliver it at least **60 days** before the intended move.

*Exceptions:*
- If the relocating person could not reasonably have known enough information to complete the form in time to give 60 days' notice, s/he must give notice within **five days** after learning the information.
- If the relocating person is relocating to a domestic violence shelter or moving to avoid a clear, immediate, and unreasonable risk to health or safety, notice may be delayed **21 days**.
- If information is protected under a court order or the address confidentiality program, it may be withheld from the notice.
- A relocating person who believes that giving notice would put her/himself or a child at unreasonable risk of harm, may ask the court for permission to leave things out of the notice or to be allowed to move without giving notice. Use form *Motion to Limit Notice of Intent to Move with Children (Ex Parte)* (FL Relocate 702).

The *Notice of Intent to Move with Children* can be delivered by having someone personally serve the other party or by any form of mail that requires a return receipt.

If the relocating person wants to change the *Parenting Plan* because of the move, s/he must deliver a proposed *Parenting Plan* together with the *Notice*.

### Move within the _same_ school district

If the move is within the _same_ school district, the relocating person still has to let the other parent know. However, the notice does not have to be served personally or by mail with a return receipt. Notice to the other party can be made in any reasonable way. No specific form is required.

### Warning! If you do not notify…

A relocating person who does not give the required notice may be found in contempt of court. If that happens, the court can impose sanctions. Sanctions can include requiring the relocating person to bring the children back if the move has already happened, and ordering the relocating person to pay the other side's costs and lawyer's fees.

### Right to object

A person who has court-ordered time with the children can object to a move to a different school district and/or to the relocating person's proposed _Parenting Plan_. If the move is within the same school district, the other party doesn't have the right to object to the move, but s/he may ask to change the _Parenting Plan_ if there are adequate reasons under the modification law (RCW 26.09.260).

An objection is made by filing the _Objection about Moving with Children and Petition about Changing a Parenting/Custody Order (Relocation)_ (form FL Relocate 721). File your _Objection_ with the court and serve a copy on the relocating person and anyone else who has court-ordered time with the children. Service of the _Objection_ must be by personal service or by mailing a copy to each person by any form of mail that requires a return receipt. The _Objection_ must be filed and served no later than **30 days** after the _Notice of Intent to Move with Children_ was received.

### Right to move

During the 30 days after the _Notice_ was served, the relocating person may not move to a different school district with the children unless s/he has a court order allowing the move.

After the 30 days, if no _Objection_ is filed, the relocating person may move with the children without getting a court order allowing the move.

After the 30 days, if an _Objection_ has been filed, the relocating person may move with the children **pending** the final hearing on the _Objection_ **unless**:

- The other party gets a court order saying the children cannot move, or
- The other party has scheduled a hearing to take place no more than 15 days after the date the _Objection_ was served on the relocating person. (However, the relocating person may ask the court for an order allowing the move even though a hearing is pending if the relocating person believes that s/he or a child is at unreasonable risk of harm.)

The court may make a different decision about the move at a final hearing on the _Objection_.

### Parenting Plan after move

If the relocating person served a proposed _Parenting Plan_ with the _Notice_, **and** if no _Objection_ is filed within 30 days after the _Notice_ was served (or if the parties agree):

- Both parties may follow that proposed plan without being held in contempt of the _Parenting Plan_ that was in place before the move. However, the proposed plan cannot be enforced by contempt unless it has been approved by a court.
- Either party may ask the court to approve the proposed plan. Use form _Ex Parte_

*Motion for Final Order Changing Parenting Plan – No Objection to Moving with Children* (FL Relocate 706).

### Forms

You can find forms about moving with children at:
- The Washington State Courts' website: *www.courts.wa.gov/forms*,
- Washington LawHelp: *www.washingtonlawhelp.org*, or
- The Superior Court Clerk's office or county law library (for a fee).

*(This is a summary of the law. The complete law is in RCW 26.09.430 through 26.09.480.)*

## 14. Other

_____

## 15. Proposal

[ ] Does not apply. This is a court order.

[ ] This is a **proposed** (requested) parenting plan. *(The parent/s requesting this plan must read and sign below.)*

I declare under penalty of perjury under the laws of the state of Washington that this plan **was proposed** in good faith and that the information in section **3** above is true.

▶ *John Doe*      *Somewhere, WA*
Parent requesting plan signs here     Signed at *(city and state)*

▶ _____     _____
Other parent requesting plan (if agreed) signs here     Signed at *(city and state)*

## 16. Court Order

[X] Does not apply. This is a proposal.

[ ] This is a court order (if signed by a judge or commissioner below).

**Findings of Fact** – Based on the pleadings and any other evidence considered:

The Court adopts the statements in section **3** (Reasons for putting limitations on a parent) as its findings.

[ ] The Court makes additional findings which are:
- [ ] contained in an order or findings of fact entered at the same time as this *Parenting Plan*.
- [ ] attached as Exhibit A as part of this *Parenting Plan*.
- [ ] other: _____

**Conclusions of Law** – This *Parenting Plan* is in the best interest of the children.

[ ] Other: _____

**Order** – The parties must follow this *Parenting Plan*.

_____     ▶ _____
Date     Judge or Commissioner signs here

DEVELOPING A PARENTING PLAN

> **Warning!** If you do not follow this *Parenting Plan*, the court may find you in contempt (RCW 26.09.160). You still have to follow this *Parenting Plan* even if the other parent doesn't.
>
> Violation of **residential** provisions of this order with actual knowledge of its terms is punishable by contempt of court and may be a criminal offense under RCW 9A.40.060(2) or 9A.40.070(2). Violation of this order may subject a violator to arrest.

**If this is a court order, the parties and/or their lawyers (and any GAL) sign below.**

This order *(check any that apply):*
[ ] is an agreement of the parties.
[X] is presented by me.
[ ] may be signed by the court without notice to me.

▶ *John Doe*
―――――――――――――――――――――――
*Petitioner or lawyer signs here + WSBA #*

*John Doe*
―――――――――――――――――――――――
Print **Name**                              Date

This order *(check any that apply):*
[ ] is an agreement of the parties.
[ ] is presented by me.
[ ] may be signed by the court without notice to me.

▶
―――――――――――――――――――――――
*Other party or lawyer signs here + WSBA #*

―――――――――――――――――――――――
Print **Name**                              Date

This order *(check any that apply):*
[ ] is an agreement of the parties.
[ ] is presented by me.
[ ] may be signed by the court without notice to me.

▶
―――――――――――――――――――――――
*Respondent or lawyer signs here + WSBA #*

―――――――――――――――――――――――
Print **Name**                              Date

This order *(check any that apply):*
[ ] is an agreement of the parties.
[ ] is presented by me.
[ ] may be signed by the court without notice to me.

▶
―――――――――――――――――――――――
*Other party or Guardian ad Litem signs here*

―――――――――――――――――――――――
Print **Name**                              Date

**Superior Court of Washington, County of** _____

In re parentage / parenting and support:

Petitioner/s *(person/s who started this case):*

_John Doe_

And Respondent/s *(other party/parties):*

_Jane Doe_

No. _____

Motion for Temporary Family Law Order (MTTO)

[ ] and Restraining Order (MTTMO)

# Motion for Temporary Family Law Order
# [ ] and Restraining Order

*Use this form for unmarried parents (parentage) cases only. For other cases, use FL Divorce 223, FL Non-Parent 423, or FL Modify 623, depending on the type of case.*

---

**To both parties:**

**Deadline!** Your papers must be filed and served by the deadline in your county's Local Court Rules, or by the State Court Rules if there is no local rule. Court Rules and forms are online at www.courts.wa.gov.

If you want the court to consider your side, you **must**:
- File your original documents with the Superior Court Clerk; AND
- Give the Judge/Commissioner a copy of your papers (if required by your county's Local Court Rules); AND
- Have a copy of your papers served on all other parties or their lawyers; AND
- Go to the hearing.

Read your county's Local Court Rules, if any.

Bring proposed orders to the hearing.

**To the person filing this motion:**

You must schedule a hearing on this motion. You may use the Notice of Hearing (form FL All Family 185) unless your county's Local Court Rules require a different form. Contact the court for scheduling information.

**To the person receiving this motion:**

If you do not agree with the requests in this motion, file a statement (using form FL All Family 135, *Declaration*) explaining why the court should not approve those requests. You may file other written proof supporting your side, and propose your own *Parenting Plan, Residential Schedule,* or *Child Support Worksheets*.

---

RCW 26.26A.470
Mandatory Form *(03/2020)*
**FL Parentage 323**

Motion for Temporary
Family Law Order

DEVELOPING A PARENTING PLAN

**1.** My name is: _____John Doe_____. I ask the court for temporary orders approving the requests listed below.

**2. Children**

[ ] No request.

[ ] I want these children under 18 listed below to be included in the court's orders:

| Child's name | Age | Child's name | Age |
|---|---|---|---|
| 1. Jay Doe | 9 | 4. | |
| 2. | | 5. | |
| 3. | | 6. | |

**3. Active duty military**

*(The **federal** Servicemembers Civil Relief Act covers:*
- *Army, Navy, Air Force, Marine Corps, and Coast Guard members on active duty;*
- *National Guard or Reserve members under a call to active service for more than 30 days in a row; and*
- *commissioned corps of the Public Health Service and NOAA.*

*The **state** Service Members' Civil Relief Act covers those service members listed above who are either stationed in or residents of Washington state, and their dependents, except for the commissioned corps of the Public Health Service and NOAA.)*

[ ] None of the other parties are covered by the state or federal Servicemembers' Civil Relief Acts.

[ ] *(Name):* _____
is covered by the [ ] state [ ] federal Servicemembers Civil Relief Act.

  [ ] *For persons covered only by the **state** act* – Military duty may keep the service member or dependent from responding or coming to the hearing on this motion. I ask the court to approve temporary orders even if the covered person asks for a stay or doesn't respond. It would be very unfair (a manifest injustice) not to make temporary orders now because: _____
  _____
  _____

**4. Care and safety of children** *(check all that apply)*

[ ] No request.

[x] Approve the *Parenting Plan* (form FL All Family 140) or *Residential Schedule* (form FL Parentage 304) **proposed by** *(check one):* [x] me [ ] *(name):* _____John Doe_____.

[x] Order *(name):* _____Jane Doe_____ not to take the children listed in **2** out of Washington State.

[ ] Appoint a person to investigate and report to the court about what is in the children's best interest, and order who will pay this person's fees. This person should be a/n *(check one):*

[ ] Guardian ad Litem (GAL) or Evaluator/Investigator as chosen by the court.
[ ] Guardian ad Litem (GAL).
[ ] Evaluator/Investigator.
[ ] *(Name):* _____

[ ] A *Sexual Assault Allegation* form has been filed saying the child was conceived by a sexual assault. The fact-finding hearing on this allegation has not happened yet.

   [ ] No residential time or decision making should be ordered until after the fact-finding hearing.
   [ ] I have a bonded and dependent relationship with the child that is parental in nature. It is in the child's best interests to order residential time or decision making now.

[ ] Other: _____
_____
_____

## 5. Provide support

[X] No request.

[ ] Order child support according to the Washington state child support schedule.

## 6. Pay fees and costs

[X] No request.

[ ] Order *(name):* _____ to:
   [ ] Pay my lawyer's fees for this case. *Amount:* $ _____
       Make payments to *(name):* _____
   [ ] Pay other professional fees and costs for this case. *Amount:* $ _____
       to *(name):* _____
       for *(purpose):* _____

[ ] Based on the Sexual Assault Allegation, award lawyer's fees consistent with RCW 26.09.140. RCW 26.26.760(12).
   Order *(name):* _____ to:
   Pay my lawyer's fees for this case. *Amount:* $ _____
   Make payments to *(name):* _____

## 7. Restraining Order

[X] No request.

[ ] The Court already signed a *Restraining Order* on *(date):* _____ in this case.
   [ ] I am not asking the court to make any changes to this *Restraining Order*.
   [ ] I ask the Court to remove (terminate) this *Restraining Order*.
   [ ] I ask the Court to change this *Restraining Order* as follows *(specify):*
   _____

[ ] I ask the Court for a *Restraining Order* (form FL All Family 150) that orders *(name/s):* _____ to obey the restraints and orders checked below. *(Check all that apply; also check the "and Restraining Order" boxes in the form titles on page 1):*

[ ] **Do not disturb** – Do not disturb my peace or the peace of any child listed in **2**.

[ ] **Stay away** – Do not go onto the grounds of or enter my home, workplace or school, and the daycare or school of any child listed in **2**.

  [ ] Also, do not knowingly go or stay within _____ feet of my home, workplace or school, or the daycare or school of any child listed in **2**.

[ ] **Do not hurt or threaten**
  - Do not assault, harass, stalk, or molest me or any child listed in **2**; and
  - Do not use, try to use, or threaten to use physical force against me or the children that would reasonably be expected to cause bodily injury.

  > *Warning!* *If the court makes this order and the parties are intimate partners, the court must consider if weapons restrictions are required by state law; federal law may also prohibit the Restrained Person from possessing firearms or ammunition.*

  [ ] **Intimate Partner:** The Restrained Person and the Protected Person are/were intimate partners because they are *(check all that apply):*
    [ ] current or former spouses or domestic partners, or parents of a child-in-common.
    [ ] age 16 or older and are/were in a dating relationship, and are currently residing together or resided together in the past.
    [ ] age 16 or older and are/were in a dating relationship, but have *never* resided together.

[ ] **Prohibit weapons and order surrender**
  - Do not access, possess or obtain any firearms, other dangerous weapons, or concealed pistol licenses until the Order ends, and
  - Immediately surrender any firearms, other dangerous weapons, and any concealed pistol licenses that he/she possesses to *(check one):* [ ] the police chief or sheriff. [ ] his/her lawyer. [ ] other person *(name):* _____.

[ ] **Other:** _____
_____
_____

## 8. Other temporary orders

[X] No request.

[ ] *(Specify):* _____
_____
_____

## Reasons for my requests

**9. Why are you asking the court for the orders you checked above? (Explain):**

- If you need additional space use the *Declaration* form FL All Family 135.
- If you are asking for a parenting plan or residential schedule, also fill out the *Information for Temporary Parenting Plan*, form FL All Family 139, and a proposed *Parenting Plan*, form FL All Family 140, or *Residential Schedule*, form FL Parentage 304.
- If you are asking for child support, also fill out the *Child Support Worksheets* and *Financial Declaration*, form FL All Family 131, and file the required financial records. If you or anyone else has ever received public assistance for any child in this case, also fill out the *Public Assistance Declaration*, form FL All Family 132.
- If you are asking to prohibit weapons or order surrender, give your reasons at the end of this section.
- If you are asking to change an earlier temporary order, give the date of the earlier order and explain how circumstances have changed since then.

I am filling this order because I am a father and I have not seen my child in 3 months. I feel a child needs his father in his life.

[ ] **Reasons for "Prohibit weapons and order surrender" request** (check all that apply):

[ ] *(Name):* _____ has used, displayed, or threatened to use a firearm or other dangerous weapon in a felony. *(Describe):*
_____
_____

[ ] *(Name):* _____ previously committed an offense making him or her ineligible to possess a firearm under RCW 9.41.040. *(Describe):*
_____
_____

[ ] *(Name):* _____'s possession of firearm presents a serious and imminent threat (harm that may happen immediately) to public health or safety, or to the health or safety of any individual. *(Describe):*
_____
_____

**Person asking for this order fills out below:**

I declare under penalty of perjury under the laws of the state of Washington that the facts I have provided on this form are true.

Signed at *(city and state):* __Somewhere, WA__    Date: __9/27/19__

▶ __John Doe__                    __John Doe__
*Person asking for this order signs here*    *Print name here*

I agree to accept legal papers for this case at *(check one):*

[ ] my lawyer's address, listed below.

[x] the following address *(this does **not** have to be your home address):*

__777 Lane St.__          __Somewhere__       __WA__  __99999__
*street address or PO box*        *city*           *state*   *zip*

> Note: You and the other party/ies may agree to accept legal papers by email under Civil Rule 5 and local court rules.

*(If this address changes before the case ends, you **must** notify all parties and the court clerk in writing. You may use the Notice of Address Change form (FL All Family 120). You must also update your Confidential Information form (FL All Family 001) if this case involves parentage or child support.)*

**Lawyer (if any) fills out below:**

▶ _____    _____    _____
*Lawyer signs here*          *Print name and WSBA No.*       *Date*

_____
*Lawyer's street address or PO box*     *city*       *state*   *zip*

Email *(if applicable):* _____

> **Warning!** Documents filed with the court are available for anyone to see unless they are sealed. Financial, medical, and confidential reports, as described in General Rule 22, **must** be sealed so they can only be seen by the court, the other party, and the lawyers in your case. Seal those documents by filing them separately, using a *Sealed* cover sheet (form FL All Family 011, 012, or 013). You may ask for an order to seal other documents.

**Superior Court of Washington, County of** _____

In re:

Petitioner/s *(person/s who started this case)*:
____*John Doe*_____

And Respondent/s *(other party/parties)*:
____*Jane Doe*_____

No. _____

Information for Temporary Parenting Plan (DCLSPP)

# Information for Temporary Parenting Plan

*The court needs the information below to order a temporary parenting plan. You may attach pages to this form if you need more space. You may fill out a separate form for each child if the information is different for each child.*

1. My name is: ____*John Doe*_____.

2. The information on this form is about:

| Child's name | Age | Child's name | Age |
|---|---|---|---|
| 1. *Jay Doe* | *9* | 4. | |
| 2. | | 5. | |
| 3. | | 6. | |

3. List the people the children have lived with in the last 12 months:

| Who the children lived with *(names)* | Where *(county/state)*? | For how long? |
|---|---|---|
| *Jane Doe* | *King/WA* | *9 years* |
| | | |
| | | |
| | | |

RCW 26.09.194(1)
Mandatory Form *(05/2016)*
FL All Family 139

Information for Temporary Parenting Plan

# DEVELOPING A PARENTING PLAN

**4.** Describe **your** involvement with the children's daily needs:

|   |   | Yes | No |
|---|---|---|---|
| a. | I have a loving and stable relationship with the children. | ☒ | ☐ |
| b. | I take care of the children's daily needs, such as feeding, clothing, physical care and grooming, supervision, doctor/dentist visits, day care, and other activities for the children. | ☐ | ☒ |
| c. | I attend to the children's education, including any necessary remedial or other education. | ☐ | ☒ |
| d. | I help the children to develop age-appropriate social relationships. | ☒ | ☐ |
| e. | I use good judgment to protect the children's well-being. | ☒ | ☐ |
| f. | I provide financial support for the children, such as housing, food, clothes, child care, health insurance, and other basic needs. | ☒ | ☐ |

*Explain and give examples for each answer above:*
A. I show my son love by expressing it
B. Child does not live with me
C. I sit and do homework with my son
D. I make sure my son is doing activities for his age
E. I make sure that my son is always in a safe place
F. I give the mother 200$ a month

**5.** List your **current** work schedule below, if any:

| Monday | Tuesday | Wed. | Thursday | Friday | Saturday | Sunday |
|---|---|---|---|---|---|---|
| 9-5 | 9-5 | 9-5 | 9-5 | 9-5 |   |   |

How long has this work schedule been in place? *(Check one):*

☒ For the past 12 months or longer.

☐ For **less** than 12 months, since *(date)*: _____. Before then, I had the work schedule listed below:

| Monday | Tuesday | Wed. | Thursday | Friday | Saturday | Sunday |
|--------|---------|------|----------|--------|----------|--------|
|        |         |      |          |        |          |        |

**6.** Describe the **other parent's** involvement with the children's daily needs:

| | The other parent *(name)*: _____Jane Doe_____ | Yes | No |
|---|---|---|---|
| a. | Has a loving and stable relationship with the children. | ☒ | ☐ |
| b. | Takes care of the children's daily needs, such as feeding, clothing, physical care and grooming, supervision, doctor/dentist visits, day care, and other activities for the children. | ☒ | ☐ |
| c. | Attends to the children's education, including any necessary remedial or other education. | ☒ | ☐ |
| d. | Helps the children to develop age-appropriate social relationships. | ☒ | ☐ |
| e. | Uses good judgment to protect the children's well-being. | ☒ | ☐ |
| f. | Provides financial support for the children, such as housing, food, clothes, child care, health insurance, and other basic needs. | ☒ | ☐ |

*Explain and give examples for each answer above:* _____
 Mother shows love by expressing it
 Mother makes sure child has everything he needs
 Mother is involved with all school matters
 Mother takes son around age-appropriate kids
 Mother makes sure kid is safe
 Mother works to provide

DEVELOPING A PARENTING PLAN    105

**7.** List the other parent's **current** work schedule below, if any:

| Monday | Tuesday | Wed. | Thursday | Friday | Saturday | Sunday |
|--------|---------|------|----------|--------|----------|--------|
| 8-5 | 8-5 | 8-5 | 8-5 | 8-5 | | |

How long has this work schedule been in place? *(Check one):*

☒ For the past 12 months or longer.

☐ For **less** than 12 months, since *(date):* _____. Before then, the other parent had the work schedule listed below:

| Monday | Tuesday | Wed. | Thursday | Friday | Saturday | Sunday |
|--------|---------|------|----------|--------|----------|--------|
| | | | | | | |

**8.** List the **children's** schedule below, including school, childcare, and other activities:

| Monday | Tuesday | Wed. | Thursday | Friday | Saturday | Sunday |
|--------|---------|------|----------|--------|----------|--------|
| school 8-3 | school 8-3 | school 8-3 | school 8-3 | school 8-3 | play | play |

**9.** Abandonment, abuse, domestic violence, sex offense, or other serious problems *(RCW 26.09.191)*

☒ Does not apply. There are no abandonment, abuse, domestic violence, sex offense, or other serious problems that affect the children in this case.

☐ *(Check one):* ☐ The other parent's  ☐ My parenting time and decision-making should be limited for the reasons listed in my proposed *Parenting Plan,* section **3.a.**

*Explain and give examples supporting those reasons for limitations:* _____

_____
_____
_____
_____
_____
_____
_____

**10.** Any other information the court needs to make a decision about a temporary *Parenting Plan*:

_____
_____
_____
_____
_____

I declare under penalty of perjury under the laws of the state of Washington that the facts I have provided on this form (and any **attachments**) are true. ☐ I have attached *(number)* ___ pages.

Signed at *(city and state)*: _____Somewhere, WA_____     Date: __9/27/19__

▶ *John Doe*                              John Doe
Sign here                                 Print name

> ***Warning!*** Documents filed with the court are available for anyone to see unless they are sealed. Financial, medical, and confidential reports, as described in General Rule 22, **must** be sealed so they can only be seen by the court, the other party, and the lawyers in your case. Seal those documents by filing them separately, using a *Sealed* cover sheet (form FL All Family 011, 012, or 013). You may ask for an order to seal other documents.

## SUPERIOR COURT WASHINGTON, COUNTY OF KING

| | |
|---|---|
| _____ vs. _____ | CASE NO. _____ KNT |
| | NOTICE OF COURT DATE<br>FAMILY LAW COMISSIONERS- KENT<br>(Clerk's Action Required) (NTMTDK) |

My name is: _____. ☐ I do not have an attorney, OR

☐ I am counsel for _____, WSBA #_____.

The court can contact me at: _____, _____
                                                 (email address)                 (phone)

The court can contact the other party at: _____, _____
                                                               (email address)                (phone)

I am asking the court to hear the following Motion(s):

1. _____ filed (date) _____

2. _____ filed (date) _____

3. _____ filed (date) _____

4. _____ filed (date) _____

The [ ] Petitioner [ ] Respondent will require interpreter services in (language) _____

**The date I have picked from** https://kingcounty.gov/courts/clerk/calendars.aspx

**is: Date:** _____ **Time:** _____

    You must pick an available date that is at least fourteen (14) calendar days after you file this form with the clerk's office AND serve the other party. (Note: for Summary Judgment Motions, it is 28 days, not 14.) Once you have found an available date, fill out the table below.

    **Important**: This court date is not guaranteed. If you choose a date with limited remaining hearings, someone may take the last slot before you can. Also, you must **file a Submission List**: or your hearing will not go forward. See the notice section on page 2.

| |
|---|
| **To:** _____ **(Name of Other Party)** |
| **A court date has been scheduled on the above motion for:** |
|    **Date:** _____. |
|    **Where:** <u>401 4th Avenue N, Kent, WA 98032.</u>_____. |
|             *Important!* Hearings are by phone or video until further notice. See notices below. |
|    **Time/Day of the Week:** ☐ Family Law Motion **1:30 p.m.** (check one below) |
|                     ☐ Attorney Calendar: Mon. Tues. or Thurs. *(if one or more parties have an attorney)* |
|                     ☐ Self-Represented Calendar: Wed or Fri. *(if both parties are self-represented)* |
|                     ☐ Motions without oral argument (by agreement only) |

Sign: _____ Date: _____

<u>Self-represented parties only:</u> I want to receive documents from the other party at:
☐ the email address above or ☐ this address: _____.

Fill out a box for each party who needs to be informed about this court date (including any Guardian Ad Litem, CASA, or Deputy Prosecuting Attorney, with Family Support Unit).
**You** must serve a copy of this form, with all motion documents, on all of these parties.

| | |
|---|---|
| Name_____<br>WSBA# _____ Attorney for:_____<br>Service Address:_____<br>City, State, Zip_____<br>Email Address: _____<br>Telephone #: _____ | Name_____<br>WSBA# _____ Attorney for:_____<br>Service Address:_____<br>City, State, Zip_____<br>Email Address: _____<br>Telephone #: _____ |
| Name_____<br>WSBA# _____ Attorney for:_____<br>Service Address:_____<br>City, State, Zip_____<br>Email Address: _____<br>Telephone #: _____ | Name_____<br>WSBA# _____ Attorney for:_____<br>Service Address:_____<br>City, State, Zip_____<br>Email Address: _____<br>Telephone #: _____ |

### IMPORTANT NOTICES REGARDING FAMILY LAW CASES

**PICKING A HEARING DATE:** The family law motions calendar has a limited number of spaces available. Prior to filing this notice, you must visit https://kingcounty.gov/courts/clerk/calendars.aspx to find an available court date. If you attempt to schedule a motion on a date that is full you will be contacted and will be required to reschedule your hearing.

NOTICE OF COURT DATE – KENT COURTHOUSE ONLY
NTMTDK-FL-CKNT 08/26/2020
www.kingcounty.gov/courts/scforms

**RESPONSE:** If you do not agree with the motion, you must file a response. Your response **must be in writing** and must be delivered no later than 12:00 p.m. (noon), five (5) court days (not including court holidays) before the court date. Your response, and submission list (see below) must be delivered to:
1) The Superior Court Clerk via e-Filing or in-person at Room 2C.
2) All parties or their attorney.

**REPLY:** the person who scheduled the court date can reply, in writing, to the response. The reply and submission list are due by noon three (3) court days prior to the hearing.

**SUBMISSION LIST/CONFIRMATION:** Each party must file a submission list. The Submission List form can be found at: https://kingcounty.gov/courts/clerk/calendars.aspx. The Submission List is a list of the documents you want the court to consider. The party filing the motion must submit the list 3 court days prior to the hearing (reply deadline). The responding party must submit the list 5 court days prior to the hearing (response deadline). **The person filing the motion must timely file this list or the hearing will not move forward (be confirmed).**

**SWORN STATEMENTS NECESSARY:** Any statements of a party or witness must be signed, dated and sworn to under penalty of perjury and must contain the state and city where signed.

**VIRTUAL HEARINGS MAY BE REQUIRED:** All family law motions hearings are being conducted by phone or video until further notice. Check the family law website for the latest information. You must include the phone number and email address you want the court to use on the Submission List. If you do not turn in a Submission List, or the court cannot reach you, the hearing may be conducted without you or may be stricken.

**WITHOUT ORAL ARGUMENT:** If you are scheduling motion without oral argument, all parties must agree. You must submit proof of the agreement with your motion.

This is only a partial summary of the family law local rules. All parties are advised to consult with an attorney.

## PIERCE COUNTY SUPERIOR COURT, STATE OF WASHINGTON

_____   )
_____   )
              Plaintiff(s),   )
  vs.   )  Case No._____
                 )
_____   )  **NOTE FOR MOTION DOCKET**
_____   )
              Defendant(s).   )

**TO THE CLERK OF THE SUPERIOR COURT:**

NAME _____ WSB#_____
ADDRESS _____ ATTORNEY FOR_____
_____ PHONE_____
        (Please note additional attorneys on an attached page)

Please take notice that the undersigned will bring on for hearing a motion for:
_____

The hearing is requested to be held during the regular motion calendar on:

| DATE REQUESTED FOR HEARING/MOTION |
|---|
| _____ at 9:00 am |

Nature of Case:_____

Dated:_____   Signed:_____

NAME _____ WSB#_____
ADDRESS _____ ATTORNEY FOR_____
_____ PHONE_____

**THE ABOVE INFORMATION MUST BE COMPLETED AND SIGNED**

FORMS\MOTIONNOTE3-2001.DAC

## Superior Court of Washington
## County of

In re the Marriage of:

*John Doe*

                    Petitioner,

and

*Jane Doe*

                      Respondent.

No.

**Motion and Declaration for Temporary Order (MTAF)**

### I. Motion

Based on the declaration below, the undersigned moves the court for a temporary order which:

[ ]     orders temporary maintenance.

[ ]     orders child support as determined pursuant to the Washington State Support Schedule.

[X]     approves the parenting plan which is proposed by the [X] husband [ ] wife.

[ ]     restrains or enjoins the [ ] husband [ ] wife from transferring, removing, encumbering, concealing or in any way disposing of any property except in the usual course of business or for the necessities of life and requiring each party to notify the other of any extraordinary expenditures made after the order is issued.

[ ]     restrains or enjoins the [ ] husband [ ] wife from disturbing the peace of the other party or of any child.

[ ]     restrains or enjoins the [ ] husband [ ] wife from going onto the grounds of or entering the home, work place or school of the other party or the day care or school of the following named children: _____.

[ ]     restrains or enjoins the [ ] husband [ ] wife from knowingly coming within or knowingly remaining within _____ (distance) of the home, work place or school of the other party or the day care or school of the following children: _____.

[ ]     restrains or enjoins _____ [Name] from molesting, assaulting, harassing, or stalking _____ [Name]. (If the court orders this relief, the restrained person will be prohibited from possessing a firearm or ammunition under

federal law for the duration of the order. An exception exists for law enforcement officers and military personnel when carrying department/government-issued firearms. 18 U.S.C. § 925(a)(1).)

[X] restrains or enjoins the [ ] husband [X] wife from removing any of the children from the state of Washington.

[ ] restrains or enjoins the [ ] husband [ ] wife from assigning, transferring, borrowing, lapsing, surrendering or changing entitlement of any insurance policies of either or both parties whether medical, health, life or auto insurance.

[ ] **(If this box is checked clear and convincing reasons for this request must be presented in the declaration below.)**
requires the [ ] husband [ ] wife to surrender any deadly weapon in his or her immediate possession or control or subject to his or her immediate possession or control to the sheriff of the county having jurisdiction of this proceeding, to his or her lawyer or to a person designated by the court.

[ ] makes each party immediately responsible for their own future debts whether incurred by credit card or loan, security interest or mortgage.

[ ] divides responsibility for the debts of the parties.

[ ] authorizes the family home to be occupied by the [ ] husband [ ] wife.

[ ] orders the use of property.

[ ] requires the [ ] husband [ ] wife to vacate the family home.

[ ] requires the [ ] husband [ ] wife to pay temporary attorney's fees, other professional fees and costs in the amount of $_____ to:

[ ] appoints a guardian ad litem on behalf of the minor children.

[ ] other:

Dated: ____9/27/19____    _____*John Doe*_____
                          Signature of Moving Party or Lawyer/WSBA No.

                          _____John Doe_____
                          Print or Type Name

## II. Declaration

Temporary relief is required because:

If the surrender of deadly weapons is requested, list reasons:

[ ] If the nonmoving party is not present and:
a) is on active duty and is a National Guard member or Reservist residing in Washington, or
b) is a dependent of a National Guard member or Reservist residing in Washington on active duty,
list the reasons why this temporary order should be granted despite the absence of the other party:

I declare under penalty of perjury under the laws of the state of Washington that the foregoing is true and correct.

Signed at __Somewhere, WA__ on __9/27/19__.
[City and State]    [Date]

__John Doe__    __John Doe__
Signature of Moving Party    Print or Type Name

**Do not attach financial records, personal health care records or confidential reports to this declaration. Such records should be served on the other party and filed with the court using one of these cover sheets:**

*1) Sealed Financial Source Documents (WPF DRPSCU 09.0220) for financial records*
*2) Sealed Personal Health Care Records (WPF DRPSCU 09.0260) for health records*
*3) Sealed Confidential Report (WPF DRPSCU 09.270) for confidential reports*

**If filed separately using a cover sheet, the records will be sealed to protect your privacy (although they will be available to all parties in the case, their attorneys, court personnel and certain state agencies and boards.) See GR 22(C)(2).**

**Superior Court of Washington, County of** _____

In re parentage / parenting and support:

Petitioner/s *(person/s who started this case)*:
_____John Doe_____

_____

And Respondent/s *(other party/parties)*:
_____Jane Doe_____

_____

No. _____

Temporary Family Law Order (TFO)

[ ] Clerk's action required: **1**, **6**, **7**

# Temporary Family Law Order

*Use this form for unmarried parents (parentage) cases only. For other cases, use FL Divorce 224, FL Non-Parent 424, or FL Modify 624, depending on the type of case.*

## 1. Money Judgment Summary

[X] No money judgment is ordered.

[ ] *Summarize any money judgments in the table below.*

| Judgment for | Debtor's name *(person who must pay money)* | Creditor's name *(person who must be paid)* | Amount | Interest |
|---|---|---|---|---|
| Lawyer's fees | | | $ | $ |
| Other fees and costs | | | $ | $ |
| Other amounts *(describe):* | | | $ | $ |
| Yearly Interest Rate: _____% *(12% unless otherwise listed)* | | | | |
| **Lawyer** *(name):* | | represents *(name):* | | |
| **Lawyer** *(name):* | | represents *(name):* | | |

## 2. Findings

The *(check one):* [X] Petitioner  [ ] Respondent *(name):* _____John Doe_____
made a *Motion for Temporary Family Law Order* (form FL Parentage 323) or a *Motion for*

DEVELOPING A PARENTING PLAN 115

*Immediate Restraining Order* (form FL Parentage 321) and the court finds there is reason to approve this order.

[ ] Specific findings: _____

_____

### 3. Active duty military

*(The **federal** Servicemembers Civil Relief Act covers:*
- *Army, Navy, Air Force, Marine Corps, and Coast Guard members on active duty;*
- *National Guard or Reserve members under a call to active service for more than 30 days in a row; and*
- *commissioned corps of the Public Health Service and NOAA.*

*The **state** Service Members' Civil Relief Act covers those service members listed above who are either stationed in or residents of Washington state, and their dependents, except for the commissioned corps of the Public Health Service and NOAA.)*

[ ] None of the parties are covered by the state or federal Service Members' Civil Relief Act, **OR** no party covered by the Acts has asked for a stay.

[ ] One or more of the parties is covered by the state or federal Service Members' Civil Relief Acts and has not appeared in this case, or has asked for a stay. *(Check one):*

  [ ] The court signed the *Order re Service Members' Civil Relief Act* (form FL All Family 170) filed separately.

  [ ] The court's order about the service member's rights is in section **8** below.

[ ] Other findings: _____

_____

## ➤ The Court Orders

### 4. Care and safety of children

[ ] No request made.

[x] This order includes these children:

| | Child's name | Age | | Child's name | Age |
|---|---|---|---|---|---|
| 1. | Jay Doe | 9 | 4. | | |
| 2. | | | 5. | | |
| 3. | | | 6. | | |

[ ] The court signed the temporary *Parenting Plan* or *Residential Schedule* filed separately.

[x] (Name/s): ___Jane Doe_____
must not take the children out of Washington state.

[ ] The court will appoint the person below to investigate and report on issues affecting the children *(check one):*

  [ ] Guardian ad Litem (GAL). The court signed the *Order Appointing Guardian ad Litem for a Child* form FL All Family 146 filed separately.

[ ] Evaluator/Investigator. The court signed the *Order Appointing Parenting Evaluator/Investigator* form FL All Family 148 filed separately.

[ ] A *Sexual Assault Allegation* form has been filed saying the child was conceived by a sexual assault. The fact-finding hearing on this allegation has not happened yet:

[ ] *(Name):* _____ shall have no residential time or decision making until after the fact-finding hearing.

[ ] *(Name):* _____ has a bonded and dependent relationship with the child that is parental in nature. It is in the child's best interests to order residential time or decision making now.

[ ] Other: _____
_____
_____

> **Important!** Attach *Summary of the Law about Moving with Children* (form FL Relocate 736) if residential time is included in this order instead of a temporary *Parenting Plan*.

## 5. Provide support

[X] No request made.

[ ] Request denied.

[ ] The court signed the temporary *Child Support Order* and *Worksheets* filed separately.

[ ] Other: _____
_____

## 6. Pay fees and costs

[X] No request made.

[ ] Request denied.

[ ] Request reserved. _____

[ ] *(Name):* _____ must:

[ ] Pay the other party's lawyer fees. *Amount:* $_____
Make payments to *(name):* _____ by *(date):* _____

[ ] Pay other fees and costs. *Amount:* $_____
Make payments to *(name):* _____ by *(date):* _____
for: _____

**Money Judgment** *(check one):*

[ ] The amount/s listed above must be paid, but the court is **not** entering a money judgment at this time.

[ ] The amount/s listed above shall be entered as a money judgment. *(Summarize the money judgment in section **1** above).* The **interest rate** is 12% unless another amount is listed here. [ ] The interest rate is ____% because *(explain):* _____
_____

DEVELOPING A PARENTING PLAN

[ ] Other: _____

**7. Restraining order**

[X] No request made.

[ ] Request denied.

[ ] The court signed the temporary *Restraining Order* (form FL All Family 150) filed separately in this case number. *(Check one):*

    [ ] No bond or security is required.

    [ ] *(Name):* _____ must file a bond or post security.
        Amount: $_____ by *(date):* _____

[ ] Any earlier *Restraining Order* that restrains *(name)* _____ signed by the court in this case number is **terminated**.

*(If you check this box, also check the "Clerk's action required" box on page 1.)*

Name of law enforcement agency where the Protected Person lived when the *Restraining Order* was issued: _____

**Clerk's Action.** The court clerk must provide a copy of this *Temporary Family Law Order* to the agency listed above within one court day. The law enforcement agency must remove the earlier *Restraining Order* from the state's database as described above.

[ ] Other orders *(specify):* _____

**8. Other temporary orders (if any)**

_____
_____

**Ordered.**

_____ ▶ _____
Date                                      Judge or Commissioner

**Petitioner and Respondent or their lawyers fill out below.**

| This order *(check any that apply)*: | This order *(check any that apply)*: |
|---|---|
| [ ] is an agreement of the parties | [ ] is an agreement of the parties |
| [ ] is presented by me | [ ] is presented by me |
| [ ] may be signed by the court without notice to me | [ ] may be signed by the court without notice to me |
| ▶ *John Doe* | ▶ |
| Petitioner signs here **or** lawyer signs here + WSBA # | Respondent signs here **or** lawyer signs here + WSBA # |
| John Doe        9/27/19 | |
| Print **Name**              Date | Print **Name**             Date |

| This order *(check any that apply)*: | This order *(check any that apply)*: |
|---|---|
| [ ] is an agreement of the parties | [ ] is an agreement of the parties |
| [ ] is presented by me | [ ] is presented by me |
| [ ] may be signed by the court without notice to me | [ ] may be signed by the court without notice to me |
| ▶ | ▶ |
| Other Respondent **or** lawyer signs here + WSBA # | Other party **or** Guardian ad Litem signs here + WSBA # |
| Print **Name**              Date | Print **Name**             Date |

**Superior Court of Washington, County of** _____

In re:

Petitioner/s (*person/s who started this case*):

_____

And Respondent/s (*other party/parties*):

_____

No. _____

Proof of Personal Service
(AFSR)

# Proof of Personal Service

*Server declares:*

**1.** My name is: _____. I am **not** a party to this case. I am 18 or older.

**2. Personal Service**

I served court documents for this case to *(name of party)*: _____
by *(check one)*:

[ ] giving the documents directly to him/her.

[ ] giving the documents to *(name)*: _____,
a person of suitable age and discretion who lives at the same address as the party.

**3. Date, time, and address of service**

Date: _____ Time: _____ [ ] a.m. [ ] p.m.

Address:

_____
Number and street                                      city                state        zip

CR 4(g), RCW 4.28.080
Optional Form *(06/2020)*
FL All Family 101

Proof of Personal Service

4. **List all documents you served** *(check all that apply)*:
   *(The most common documents are listed below. Check only those documents that were served. Use the "Other" boxes to write in the title of each document you served that is not already listed.)*

| [ ] Petition to/for _____ | |
|---|---|
| [ ] Summons *(Attach a copy.)* | [ ] Notice of Hearing _____ |
| [ ] Order Setting Case Schedule | [ ] Motion for Temporary Family Law Order [ ] and Restraining Order |
| [ ] Notice Re: Military Dependent | [ ] Proposed Temporary Family Law Order |
| [ ] Proposed Parenting Plan | [ ] Motion for Immediate Restraining Order (Ex Parte) |
| [ ] Proposed Child Support Order | [ ] Immediate Restraining Order (Ex Parte) and Hearing Notice |
| [ ] Proposed Child Support Worksheets | [ ] Restraining Order |
| [ ] Sealed Financial Documents | [ ] Motion for Contempt Hearing |
| [ ] Financial Declaration | [ ] Order to Go to Court for Contempt Hearing |
| [ ] Information for Temporary Parenting Plan | [ ] Motion for Adequate Cause Decision |
| [ ] Declaration of: _____ | [ ] Notice of Intent to Move with Children (Relocation) |
| [ ] Declaration of: _____ | [ ] Objection about Moving with Children and Petition about Changing a Parenting/Custody Order (Relocation) |
| [ ] Other: _____ | [ ] Other: _____ |
| [ ] Other: _____ | [ ] Other: _____ |

5. **Fees charged for service**

   [ ] Does not apply.

   [ ] Fees: $ _____ + Mileage $ _____ = Total: $ _____

6. **Other Information** *(if any)*: _____
   _____

I declare under penalty of perjury under the laws of the state of Washington that the statements on this form are true.

Signed at *(city and state)*: _____ Date: _____

▶ _____     _____
Signature of server                    Print or type name of server

**To the party having these documents served:**

- File the original *Proof of Personal Service* with the court clerk.
- If you served a *Restraining Order* signed by the court, you must also give a copy of this *Proof of Personal Service* and a *Law Enforcement Information Sheet* to law enforcement.
- If the documents were personally served outside of Washington state, you must fill out and file form FL All Family 102 (*Declaration: Personal Service Could Not be Made in Washington*).

[ ] **To the Server:** check here if you personally served the documents *outside* Washington state. Your signature must be notarized or sworn before a court clerk.

*(For personal service in Washington state, your signature does **not** need to be notarized or sworn before a court clerk.)*

Signed and sworn to before me on *(date)*: _____.

▶ _____
Signature of notary or court clerk

_____
Print name of notary or court clerk

[ ] I am a notary public in and for the state of:
_____

My commission expires: _____

[ ] I am a court clerk in a court of record in
(county): _____

*(Print seal above.)*   (state): _____

Proof of Personal Service

Superior Court of Washington, County of _____

In re parenting and support of:

Children:

___Jay Doe___

Petitioner *(person who started this case)*:

___John Doe___

And Respondent *(other parent)*:

___Jane Doe___

No. _____

Final Order and Findings for a Parenting Plan, Residential Schedule, and/or Child Support
(JDPPCS)

[ ] Clerk's action required: **1**, **15**, **16**

# Final Order and Findings for a Parenting Plan, Residential Schedule and/or Child Support

### 1. Money Judgment Summary

[ ] No money judgment is ordered.

[ ] Summarize any money judgment from section **16** in the table below.

| Judgment for | Debtor's name *(person who must pay money)* | Creditor's name *(person who must be paid)* | Amount | Interest |
|---|---|---|---|---|
| Lawyer fees | | | $ | $ |
| Guardian ad litem fees | | | $ | $ |
| Court costs | | | $ | $ |
| Other *(specify):* | | | $ | $ |
| Yearly Interest Rate: ___% *(12% unless otherwise listed)* | | | | |
| Lawyer *(name):* | | represents *(name):* | | |
| Lawyer *(name):* | | represents *(name):* | | |

RCW 26.26B.020(7)(b)
(07/2019)
**FL Parentage 333**

**2. Court findings based on** *(check all that apply)*:

[ ] Parents' agreement.
[ ] *Order on Motion for Default* signed on *(date):* _____.
[ ] The court's decision after a contested hearing on *(date):* _____.

The following people were at the hearing *(list parents, lawyers, and any guardians ad litem):* _____
_____

## ➤ Findings & Conclusions

### 3. Children

Petitioner and Respondent are parents of the following children who will be covered by a *Parenting Plan, Residential Schedule,* and/or *Child Support Order:*

| Child's name | Age | Child's name | Age |
|---|---|---|---|
| 1. | | 4. | |
| 2. | | 5. | |
| 3. | | 6. | |

### 4. Parentage established *(Repeat this section for each child as needed.)*

[ ] **Court Order** – Parentage was established by court order for *(children's names):* _____ on *(date):* _____
by *(name of court):* _____.

[ ] **Acknowledgment of Parentage** – The Petitioner and Respondent signed an *Acknowledgment of Parentage* (Affidavit) for *(child's name):* _____
that was filed with the appropriate agency of the state of _____
on *(date):* _____.

  [ ] The mother was married or in a registered domestic partnership when the child was born (or within 300 days before). Her spouse/partner *(name):* _____
  _____ signed a *Denial of Parentage* that was filed with the appropriate agency of the state of _____
  on *(date)* _____.

### 5. Washington state deadlines for Acknowledgment of Parentage

[ ] Does not apply because parentage was established either by court order or by an *Acknowledgment of Parentage* (Affidavit) filed in in a <u>different</u> state than Washington. *(Skip to 6.)*

[ ] The *Acknowledgment of Parentage* was filed in Washington state.

  **a. Effective date** -- The *Acknowledgment of Parentage* (and *Denial*, if any) became effective (valid) on the date the child was born or the date the *Acknowledgment of Parentage* (and *Denial*, if any) was filed with the Washington State Registrar of Vital Statistics, whichever was later.

### b. Deadline to withdraw

[ ] The deadline to withdraw (rescind) the *Acknowledgment of Parentage* or *Denial* has passed because:

[ ] This case was filed **more** than 60 days from the effective date. .

[ ] This case was filed **less** than 60 days from the effective date; **but** everyone who signed the *Acknowledgment* (and *Denial*, if any) was before the court to decide an issue about the child before this case was filed.

[ ] The deadline to withdraw (rescind) the *Acknowledgment of Parentage* or *Denial* has **not** passed. The petition was filed too soon.

### c. Deadline to challenge

[ ] The deadline to challenge the *Acknowledgment of Parentage* or *Denial* has passed because it has been **more** than four years since effective date.

[ ] The deadline to challenge the *Acknowledgment of Parentage* or *Denial* has **not** passed because it has been **less** than four years since the effective date.

*Check one:*

[ ] The court will approve parenting and/or support orders for the child because the court finds:
- The child's acknowledged father is the father,
- No court has said another man is the child's father,
- There are no other open court cases to decide who the child's father is, **and**
- Notice has been given to all other men who claimed to be this child's father.

[ ] The court will **not** approve parenting and/or support orders for the child because the Petitioner failed to show *(check all that apply)*:
- [ ] The child's acknowledged father is the father.
- [ ] No court has said another man is the child's father.
- [ ] There are no other open court cases to decide who the child's father is.
- [ ] Notice has been given to all other men who claimed to be this child's father.

## 6. Acknowledgment of Parentage filed in another state

[ ] Does not apply because parentage was established either by court order or by *Acknowledgment of Parentage* filed in Washington state. *(Skip to 7.)*

[ ] The *Acknowledgment of Parentage* was filed in a different state than Washington. The *Acknowledgment (check one):*

[ ] is valid under the laws of that state.

[ ] is not valid under the laws of that state because: _____

_____
_____
_____.

7. **Notice and jurisdiction over parents**
   - Notice was given to everyone with a legal right to receive it, and
   - The court has jurisdiction over the parents in this case because *(check all that apply):*
     [ ] the Petitioner lives in Washington State.
     [ ] the Respondent lives in Washington State.
     [ ] the Respondent was personally served in this state with the *Summons* and *Petition*.
     [ ] the Respondent signed an agreement to join this *Petition* or other document agreeing that the court can decide his or her rights in this case.
     [ ] other *(specify):* _____

8. **Jurisdiction over the children** (RCW 26.27.201 – .221, .231, .261, .271)

   [ ] The court **cannot** order a parenting/custody order for the children because the court does not have jurisdiction over the children. *(Skip to 9.)*

   [ ] The court **can** order a parenting/custody order for the children because *(check all that apply; if a box applies to all of the children, you may write "the children" instead of listing names):*

   [ ] **Exclusive, continuing jurisdiction** – A Washington court has already made a custody order or parenting plan for the children, and the court still has authority to make other orders for *(children's names):* _____.

   [ ] **Home state jurisdiction** – Washington is the children's home state because *(check all that apply):*

   [ ] *(Children's names):* _____ lived in Washington with a parent or someone acting as a parent for at least the 6 months just before this case was filed, or if the children were less than 6 months old when the case was filed, they had lived in Washington with a parent or someone acting as a parent since birth.

     [ ] There were times the children were not in Washington in the 6 months just before this case was filed (or since birth if they were less than 6 months old), but those were temporary absences.

   [ ] *(Children's names):* _____ do not live in Washington right now, but Washington was the children's home state sometime in the 6 months just before this case was filed, and a parent or someone acting as a parent of the children still lives in Washington.

   [ ] *(Children's names):* _____ do not have another home state.

   [ ] **No home state or home state declined** – No court of any other state (or tribe) has the jurisdiction to make decisions for *(children's names):* _____, **or** a court in the children's home state (or tribe) decided it is better to have this case in Washington **and:**
     - The children and a parent or someone acting as a parent have ties to Washington beyond just living here; **and**
     - There is a lot of information (substantial evidence) about the children's care, protection, education and relationships in this state.

DEVELOPING A PARENTING PLAN

[ ] **Other state declined** – The courts in other states (or tribes) that might be *(children's names):* _____'s home state have refused to take this case because it is better to have this case in Washington.

[ ] **Temporary emergency jurisdiction** – Washington had temporary emergency jurisdiction over *(children's names):* _____ when the case was filed, and now has jurisdiction to make a final custody decision because:
- When the case was filed, the children were abandoned in this state, or the children were in this state and the children (or children's parent, brother or sister) was abused or threatened with abuse;
- The court signed a temporary order on *(date)* _____ saying that Washington's jurisdiction will become final if no case is filed in the children's home state (or tribe) by the time the children have been in Washington for 6 months;
- The children have now lived in Washington for 6 months; **and**
- No case concerning the children has been started in the children's home state (or tribe).

[ ] Other reason *(specify):* _____

## 9. Parenting Plan or Residential Schedule

[ ] Does not apply.

[ ] The court signed the final *Parenting Plan* or *Residential Schedule* filed separately today or on *(date):* _____.

[ ] Other findings: _____
_____

## 10. Child Support

[ ] Does not apply.

[ ] **Court Order** – The court signed the final *Child Support Order* and *Worksheets* filed separately today or on *(date):* _____.
Tax issues and post-secondary (college or vocational school) support are covered in the Child Support Order.

[ ] **Administrative Order** – The court is **not** issuing a child support order. There is an administrative child support order established by DSHS Division of Child Support (DCS) for the dependent children.

DCS child support orders do not cover tax issues or post-secondary (college or vocational school) support. Therefore, the court orders:

[ ] **Tax Issues** – The parties have the right to claim the children as their dependents for purposes of personal tax exemptions and associated tax credits on their tax forms as follows *(describe):* _____

For tax years when a non-custodial parent has the right to claim the children, the parents must cooperate to fill out and submit IRS Form 8332 in a timely manner.

> *Important!* Although the personal tax exemptions are currently suspended under federal law through tax year 2025, other tax benefits may flow from claiming a child as dependent.

[ ] **Post-secondary (college or vocational school)** –The court orders:
    [ ] A parent may ask the court for post-secondary support at a later date, but he/she must file that request before the duty to pay child support ends.
    [ ] The parents must pay for the children's post-secondary support. The parents will make a post-secondary support plan or the court will order one.
    [ ] Post-secondary support is **not** required.
    [ ] Other *(specify):* _____
[ ] Other findings: _____
_____

## 11. Protection Order

[ ] No one requested an *Order for Protection* in this case.

[ ] **Approved** – The request for an *Order for Protection* is approved. The *Order for Protection* is filed separately.

[ ] **Denied** – The request for an *Order for Protection* is denied. The *Denial Order* is filed separately.

[ ] **Renewed/Changed** – The existing *Order for Protection* filed in or combined with this case is renewed or changed as described in the following order, filed separately *(check one):*
    [ ] *Order on Renewal of Order for Protection*
    [ ] *Order Modifying/Terminating Order for Protection*

[ ] Other findings: _____
_____

## 12. Restraining Order

[ ] No one requested a *Restraining Order* in this case.

[ ] **Approved** – The request for a *Restraining Order* is approved. The *Restraining Order* is filed separately.

[ ] **Denied** – The request for a *Restraining Order* is denied.

[ ] Other findings: _____
_____

## 13. Fees and Costs

[ ] Each party should pay his/her own fees and costs.

[ ] *(Name):* _____ incurred fees and costs, and needs help to pay those fees and costs. *(Name):* _____ has the ability to help pay fees and costs and should be ordered to pay the amount as listed in the Money Judgment in section **16** below. The court finds that the amount ordered is reasonable.

[ ] Fees for a guardian ad litem (GAL) or other court-appointed professional should be paid as listed in the Money Judgment in section **16** below. The court has considered

relevant factors including each party's ability to pay, and finds the fees as ordered are reasonable.

[ ] Other findings: _____

**14. Other findings, if any**

_____
_____
_____

## ➢ *Court Orders*

**15. Decision** *(check all that apply):*

[ ] **Denied** – The court denies the *Petition*. All temporary orders are ended.

[ ] **Approved** – The court approves the *Petition*. All temporary orders are ended. The court signed the following orders filed separately:

[ ] *Parenting Plan*      [ ] *Order for Protection*
[ ] *Residential Schedule*      [ ] *Restraining Order*
[ ] *Child Support Order*
[ ] *Other orders:* _____

[ ] The guardian ad litem is discharged.

[ ] *Check this box if the court previously signed a <u>temporary</u> Restraining Order and is **not** signing a <u>final</u> Restraining Order in this case. Also check the "Clerk's action required" box in the caption on page 1.*

Name of law enforcement agency where the Protected Person lived when the *Restraining Order* was issued: _____

**To the Clerk:** Provide a copy of this Order to the agency listed above within 1 court day. The law enforcement agency must remove the <u>temporary</u> *Restraining Order* from the state's database.

**16. Money Judgment** *(summarized on page 1)*

[ ] No money judgment is ordered.

[ ] The court orders a money judgment as follows:

| Judgment for | Debtor's name *(person who must pay money)* | Creditor's name *(person who must be paid)* | Amount | Interest |
|---|---|---|---|---|
| [ ] Lawyer fees | | | $ | $ |
| [ ] Guardian ad litem fees | | | $ | $ |
| [ ] Court costs | | | $ | $ |
| [ ] Other *(specify):* | | | $ | $ |

The **interest rate** is 12% unless another amount is listed below.
[ ] The interest rate is ____% because *(explain):* _____
_____

[ ] Other: _____

## 17. Other orders, if any

_____
_____
_____

**Ordered.**

_____    ▶ _____
*Date*                              *Judge or Commissioner*

### Petitioner and Respondent or their lawyers fill out below:

This document *(check any that apply)*:          This document *(check any that apply)*:
[ ] is an agreement of the parties                [ ] is an agreement of the parties
[ ] is presented by me                            [ ] is presented by me
[ ] may be signed by the court without notice to me   [ ] may be signed by the court without notice to me

▶ _____    ▶ _____
*Petitioner signs here or lawyer signs here + WSBA #*   *Respondent signs here or lawyer signs here + WSBA #*

_____    _____
*Print Name*              *Date*    *Print Name*              *Date*

### [ ] Guardian ad Litem:

This document *(check all that apply)*:
[ ] is an agreement of the parties
[ ] is presented by me
[ ] may be signed by the court without notice to me

▶ _____    _____    _____
*GAL signs here*                      *Print name and WSBA # (if any)*    *Date*

### [ ] If any parent or child received public assistance:

The state Department of Social and Health Services (DSHS) was notified about this Order, and has reviewed and approved the following orders:
[ ] Child support              [ ] Medical support
[ ] Past due child support     [ ] Other *(specify):* _____

▶ _____    _____    _____
*Deputy Prosecutor signs here*        *Print name and WSBA #*            *Date*

RCW 26.26B.020(7)(b)    Final Order and Findings for a Parenting
(07/2019)               Plan, Res. Sched. and/or Child Support
FL Parentage 333

## Superior Court of Washington, County of _____

In re:
Petitioner/s *(person/s who started this case)*:
___John Doe___

And Respondent/s *(other party/parties)*:
___Jane Doe___

No. _____

Declaration of *(name)*: _____
(DCLR)

## Declaration of *(name)*: ___John Doe___

1. I am *(age)*: __42__ years old and I am the *(check one)*: ☒ Petitioner ☐ Respondent
   ☐ Other *(relationship to the people in this case)*: _____

2. I declare: ___That I am a father who has not seen his child in 3 months. I feel that a child needs a father and I would like to continue that with my child. I think a child needs both parents and that is the best interest for the child.___

Optional Form *(05/2016)*
FL All Family 135

Declaration
p. 1 of __

_____

_____

_____

_____

_____

_____

_____

_____

_____

_____

_____

_____

_____

_____

_____

_____

_____

_____

_____

_____

_____

_____

_____

_____

_____

*(Number any pages you attach to this Declaration. Page limits may apply.)*

I declare under penalty of perjury under the laws of the state of Washington that the facts I have provided on this form (and any attachments) are true. ☐ I have attached *(number):* ___ pages.

Signed at *(city and state):* _____  Date: _____

▶ _____     _____
Sign here                                                      Print name

> **Warning!** Documents filed with the court are available for anyone to see unless they are sealed. Financial, medical, and confidential reports, as described in General Rule 22, **must** be sealed so they can only be seen by the court, the other party, and the lawyers in your case. Seal those documents by filing them separately, using a *Sealed* cover sheet (form FL All Family 011, 012, or 013). You may ask for an order to seal other documents

## FAMILY
_____ COUNTY SUPERIOR COURT
Case Information Cover Sheet (CICS)

Case Number_____ Case Title _____

Attorney Name _____ Bar Membership Number _____

Please check one category that best describes this case for indexing purposes. Accurate case indexing not only saves time in docketing new cases, but helps in forecasting needed judicial resources. Cause of action definitions are listed on the back of this form. Thank you for your cooperation.

- ☐ ADP Adoption
- ☐ ARY At-Risk Youth
- ☐ CHN Confidential Name Change
- ☐ CIR Committed Intimate Relationship
- ☐ CNS Child in Need of Services
- ☐ CUS Child Custody
- ☐ DDP Developmental Disability
- ☐ DEP Dependency
- ☐ DFP De Facto Parentage
- ☐ DIC Dissolution of Marriage with Children
- ☐ DIN Dissolution of Marriage with No Children
- ☐ DPC Dissolution of Dom. Partnership-w/Children
- ☐ DPN Dissolution of Dom. Partnership-No Children
- ☐ EFC Extended Foster Care Services
- ☐ FJU Foreign Judgment – Domestic
- ☐ GFC Guardianship Foster Care
- ☐ INP Invalidity – Domestic Partnership
- ☐ INV Annulment – Invalidity
- ☐ MDS Modification – Support Only
- ☐ MOD 3 Domestic Modification
- ☐ MOD 5 Parentage Modification
- ☐ MSC 3 Miscellaneous Domestic
- ☐ MSC 5 Miscellaneous – Adoption
- ☐ MWA Mandatory Wage Assignment

- ☐ OSC Out-of-State Child Custody
- ☐ PAT Parentage – Parental Determination
- ☐ PPR Initial Pre-Placement Report
- ☐ PPS Parenting Plan / Child Support
- ☐ PUR Parentage (URESA/UIFSA)
- ☐ PAS Parentage Surrogacy
- ☐ RCV Relative Child Visitation
- ☐ REL Relinquishment
- ☐ RIC Reciprocal, Respondent In-County
- ☐ ROC Reciprocal, Respondent Out-of-County
- ☐ RPR Reinstatement of Parental Rights
- ☐ RVS Relative Visitation
- ☐ SEP Legal Separation
- ☐ SPD Legal Separation – Domestic Partnership
- ☐ TER 5 Termination of Parental Rights-Parentage
- ☐ TER 7 Termination of Parental Rights-Dependency
- ☐ TRU Truancy
- ☐ VYG Vulnerable Youth Guardianship

**IF YOU CANNOT DETERMINE THE APPROPRIATE CATEGORY, PLEASE DESCRIBE THE CAUSE OF ACTION BELOW.**
_____

*Please Note: Public information in court files and pleadings may be posted on a public Web site.*

## DOMESTIC RELATIONS

**Annulment--Invalidity**--Petition claiming an illegal or invalid marriage.
**Child Custody**--Petition involving the immediate charge and control of a child.
**Committed Intimate Relationship**--Petition for distribution of property from a committed intimate relationship (i.e., a stable, marital-like relationship where both parties cohabit with knowledge that a lawful marriage between them does not exist).
**De Facto Parentage**-Petition filed under RCW 26.26A.440 requesting the court for an order finding the petitioner to be the de facto parent of the child named in the petition.
**Dissolution with Children**--Petition to terminate a marriage other than annulment, with children of that marriage.
**Dissolution with no Children**--Petition to terminate a marriage other than annulment, with no children of that marriage.
**Dissolution of Domestic Partnership--With Children**--Petition to terminate a domestic partnership, other than annulment, with children of that domestic partnership.
**Dissolution of Domestic Partnership--With No Children**--Petition to terminate a domestic partnership, other than annulment, with no children of that domestic partnership.
**Foreign Judgment**--A judgment, decree, or order of a court of the United States, or any state or territory, which is entitled to full faith and credit in this state.
**Invalidity--Domestic Partnership**--Petition to invalidate a domestic partnership.
**Legal Separation**--Petition to live separate and apart.
**Legal Separation-Domestic Partnership**--Petition to live separate and apart in a domestic partnership.
**Mandatory Wage Assignment**--Petition for wage assignment.
**Modification**--Petition seeking amendment of a previous order or decree. **(MOD 3)**
**Modification: Support Only**--Petition seeking amendment of a previous order or decree regarding support.
**Out-of-State Custody**--Recording custody established out-of-state.
**Parenting Plan/Child Support**--Petition for Residential Schedule/Parenting Plan/Child Support in circumstances set forth in RCW 26.26.375.
**Reciprocal, Respondent-in-County**--Petition to enforce orders between states under URESA for respondents in the county.
**Reciprocal, Respondent-Out-of-County**--Petition to enforce orders between states under URESA for respondents out of the county.
**Relative Child Visitation** – Relatives, Grandparents--Request filed by eligible relative for visitation with a child (RCW 26.11).

## DOMESTIC VIOLENCE/ ANTIHARASSMENT

**Confidential Name Change**--Petition for name change, when domestic violence/antiharassment issues require confidentiality.

## ADOPTION/PARENTAGE (SCOMIS Case Type 5)

**Adoption**--Petition to establish a new, permanent relationship of parent and child not having that relationship.
**Confidential Intermediary**--Petition to appoint a confidential intermediary to contact the adopted person(s), birth parent(s), or other relative(s).
**Initial Pre-Placement**--An initial pre-placement report filed on a child by the DSHS prior to the filing of adoption papers.
**Modification**--Petition seeking amendment of a previous order or decree. **(MOD 5)**
**Parentage**--Petition to determine the legal status of a parent.
**Parentage Surrogacy**-Court proceedings related to provisions of surrogacy agreements.

**Paternity/URESA/UIFSA**--Petition to determine the legal status of a parent which is filed in conjunction with the reciprocal report entered under the URESA or UIFSA acts.
**Relinquishment**--Petition to relinquish a child to DSHS, an agency, or a prospective adoptive parent.
**(Title 26) Termination of Parent-Child Relationship**--Petition to terminate a parent-child relationship when parent has not executed a written consent. **(TER 5)**

## DEPENDENCY

**At-Risk Youth**--Petition to request available juvenile court services for personal or family situations that present a serious and imminent threat to the at-risk child or family (RCW 13.32A.120 or 13.32A.150).
**Child in Need of Services**--Petition to the court to allow out-of-home placement of a minor.
**Dependency**--Petition alleging a person under the age of 18 is dependent and requires court intervention to ensure his or her well-being (RCW 13.34.040). File a guardianship petition under the existing dependency action. Do not change the cause-of-action code if the dependency action results in the filing of a guardianship petition (RCW 13.34.230).Note: A termination petition should always be a new cause of action, and should not be filed under the dependency action.
**Developmental Disability Placement**--Petition for a voluntary placement agreement when the sole reason for the out-of-home placement is the child's developmental disability (RCW 74.13.350).
**Extended Foster Care Services**--Extended foster care services cases will include (1) Youth in an open dependency case who, upon turning 18 years of age, request extended foster care services under criteria set out in Chapter 332 Laws 2013; and (2) Youth whose dependency cases were dismissed at age 18 and who subsequently request extended foster care services through a voluntary placement agreement prior to turning age 19.
**Guardianship Foster Children**--Petition filed by any party to a dependency proceeding to request a guardianship be established for a child in foster care.
**Reinstatement of Parental Rights**--Petition filed by a child requesting reinstatement of the previously terminated parental rights.
**Relative Visitation**--Petition filed by a dependent child's relative, other than a child's parent, requesting reasonable visitation with the dependent child.
**Termination**--Petition for a termination of a parent and child relationship following a finding of dependency and other criteria set forth in RCW 13.34.180. A termination petition should always be a new cause of action, and should not be filed under the dependency action. **(TER 7)**
**Truancy (TRU)**--Petition to request the juvenile court to intervene on behalf of a juvenile who is unjustifiably truant from school (RCW 28A.225.030).
**Vulnerable Youth Guardianship**--Petition to appoint a guardian for vulnerable youth (18-21) who is not participating in foster care services (RCW 13.90.020).

Updated: 6/11/2020

# CHAPTER FOUR

# 4.1 Scheduling Appointments

Note: The next two sections assume you are using the Apricot and ILINX systems utilized by D.A.D.S. Seattle offices. If you are using a different system, you can modify or skip these sections as needed.

Never leave client files unattended or accessible. Client intake files must always be attended or protected under lock and key.

## Existing clients, walk-ins, or calls for appointments

- Check ILINX and Apricot to see if the client has been to D.A.D.S. before and read any service episode comments posted there.
- Confirm that there is adequate time to assist a walk-in client; otherwise, have them fill out the intake paperwork if they are a first-time visitor and set an appointment for them to return.
- When someone is calling in to possibly do a parenting plan, make sure they have the child's birth certificate—if not, they will need this to proceed. Also make sure they bring any court documentation they may have in place. Remember that a parenting plan can take a few hours, so set aside time accordingly on the calendar.

## Creating appointments on Google Calendar

1. Open Google Calendar.
2. Click the **Create** button on the left-hand side of the calendar.
3. Under **Add Title**, input the client's name, purpose for visit (CS or PP), and their phone number. Confirm the spelling of the client's name and his contact phone

number. (The number that appears on the caller ID isn't always the correct contact number.)
4. Add the location (e.g., in Washington, either Seattle or Tacoma).
5. Click on **More Options** on the bottom right corner to type in notes from your conversation to prepare the intake specialist that will be assisting the client.
Examples:

**Steve Martin, 206-444-4444 CS**
Steve has three children and wants to see about getting his CS modified due to an old order when he was making twice the income he is now. He will bring in two years' worth of tax returns and the last two months of paystubs for further review and assistance.

**Francisco Martinez, 425-777-1234, PP**
Francisco has six-year-old twin daughters and the mother's new boyfriend will not let him see his children. He will bring in a copy of their BC (birth certificate) and would like help with creating a PP (parenting plan).

6. Check the box on the right that says guests can **Modify Event.** This way, if the client calls to cancel or reschedule, anyone can make that change.
7. Under **Guests,** on the right side, you can add the staff member that may need to attend the appointment or in the corresponding office of the appointment scheduled.
8. Select **Save** in the top right-hand corner.

## 4.2 Scanning Documents

When scanning a document, it is important to decide ahead of time where you will want the document stored for future access. You may need to create a folder under DCS Authorization with the client's first and last name to save that form to that file to easily find when sending them to DCS. It may be a document that would be needed to save to the desktop for quick access as well. Determining where the document will be stored will help you when you start to scan documents into the system.

1. Complete the documents.
2. Insert the document that you would like to scan into your document scanner.
3. Save the scanned document to the appropriate file on your computer and label it for future access.

## 4.3 Telephone Guide

We encourage you to have a designated phone number for your D.A.D.S. office, whether a Google account that can be accessed by cell phone (not your personal number), or a land line.

When there are incoming calls, we recommend a professional greeting saying something like, "D.A.D.S. office, how may I help you?" It is important to try and answer every call, as each call is an opportunity to connect fathers with their children. If we can't help the caller, we may be able to refer them to someone who can.

We encourage you to set up a voicemail box to receive calls that come outside of office hours, and to return these calls in a timely manner.

# 4.4 Training Instructions for ILINX

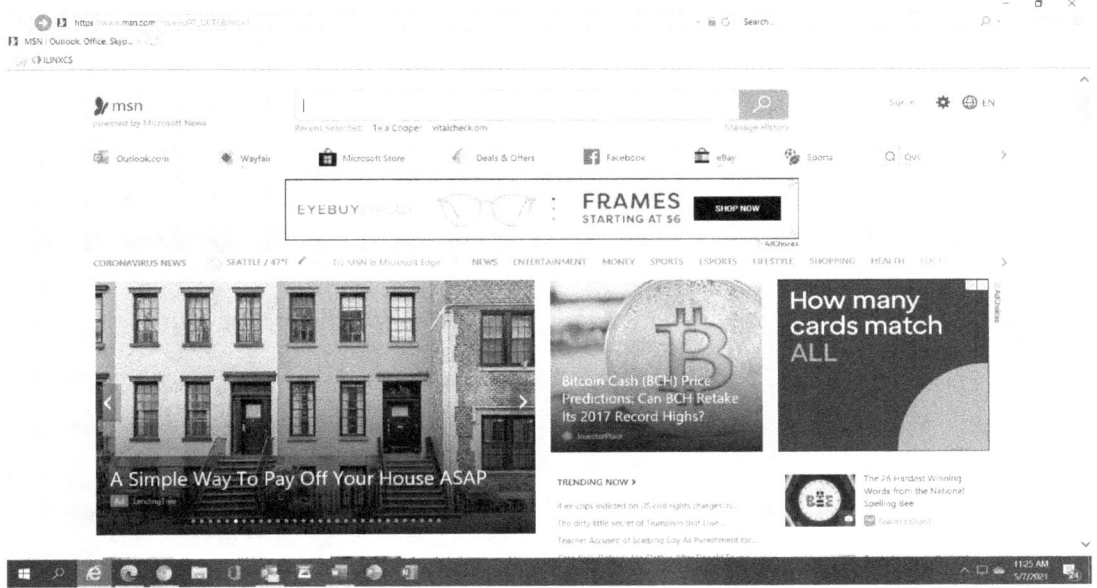

Click on the ILINKS Tab.

# 140 DOING DADS: INTAKE AND SUPPORT MANUAL

To login to **ILINKS** you need to enter your assigned username and password then click on **Sign-In Box.**

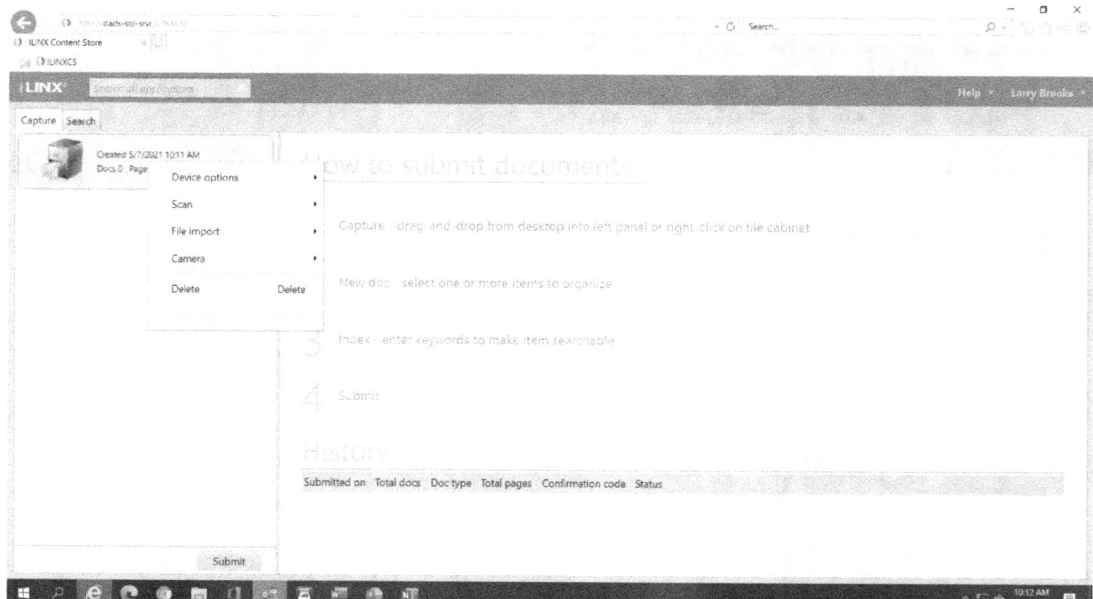

# TRAINING INSTRUCTIONS FOR ILINX

To import document into ILINKS you would click on **Capture**.

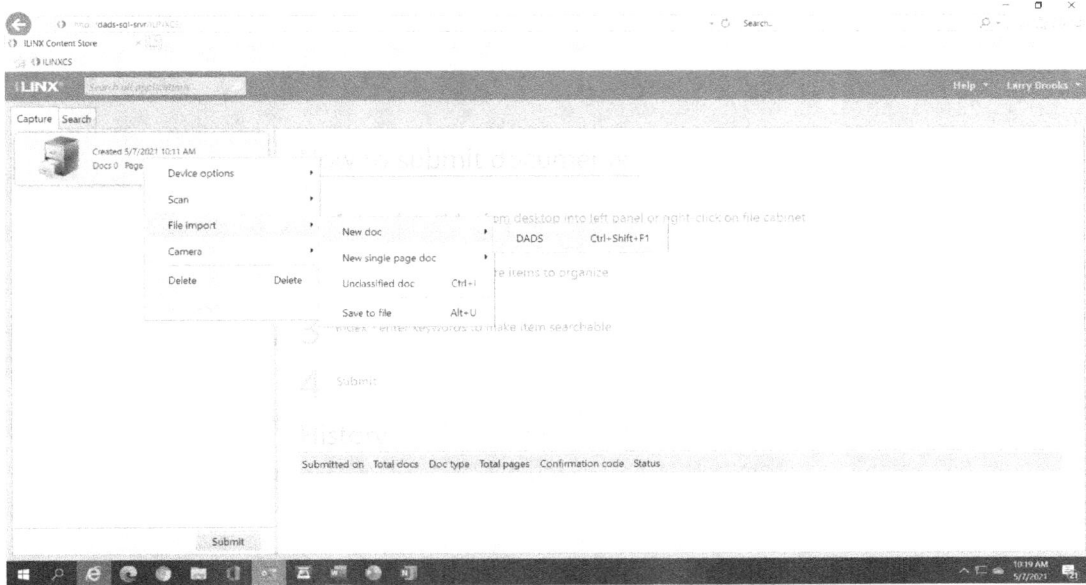

Then click on **File Import** then move cursor to the on **New Doc**, and again move cursor onto **DADS Cltri+Shift+F1** then hit Enter.

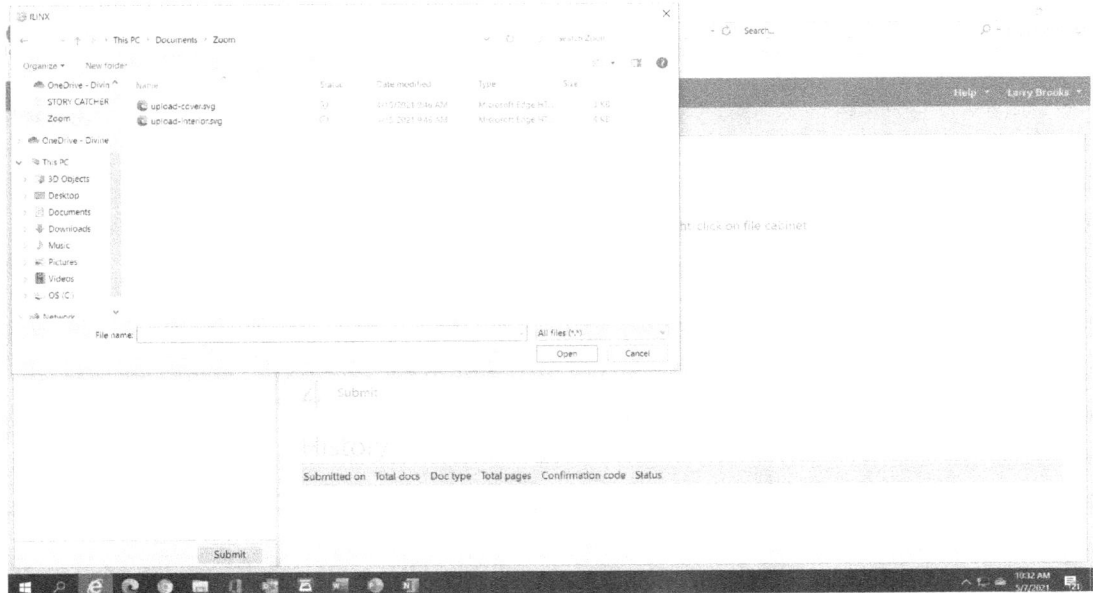

Click on the document file you want then click **Open**.

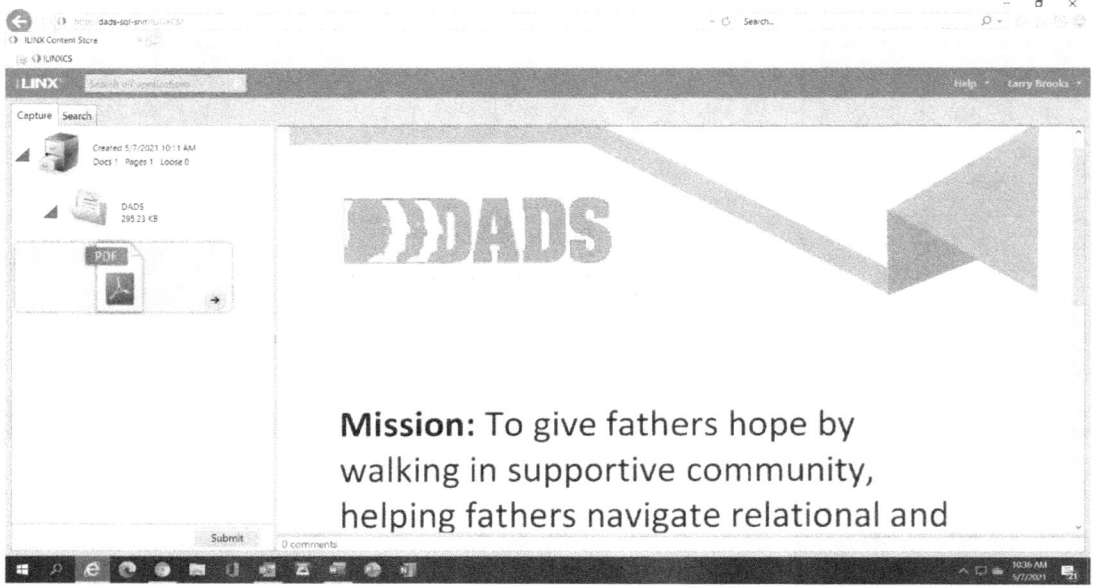

Click on the yellow arrow.

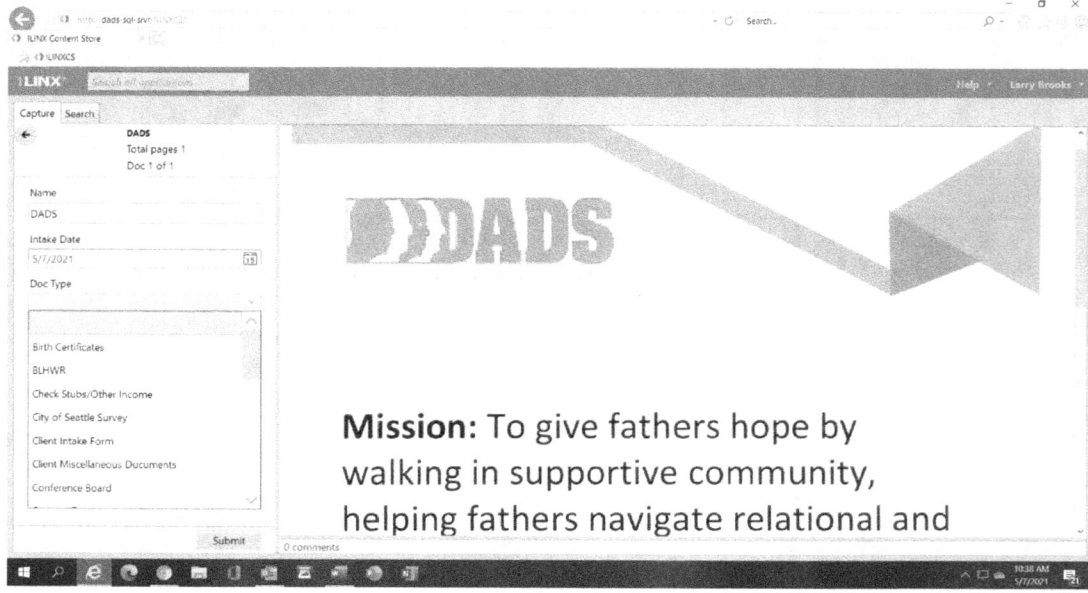

Type clients **Name**, put the clients **Intake Date**. Then click on **Doc Type** and then scroll down to appropriate doc type.

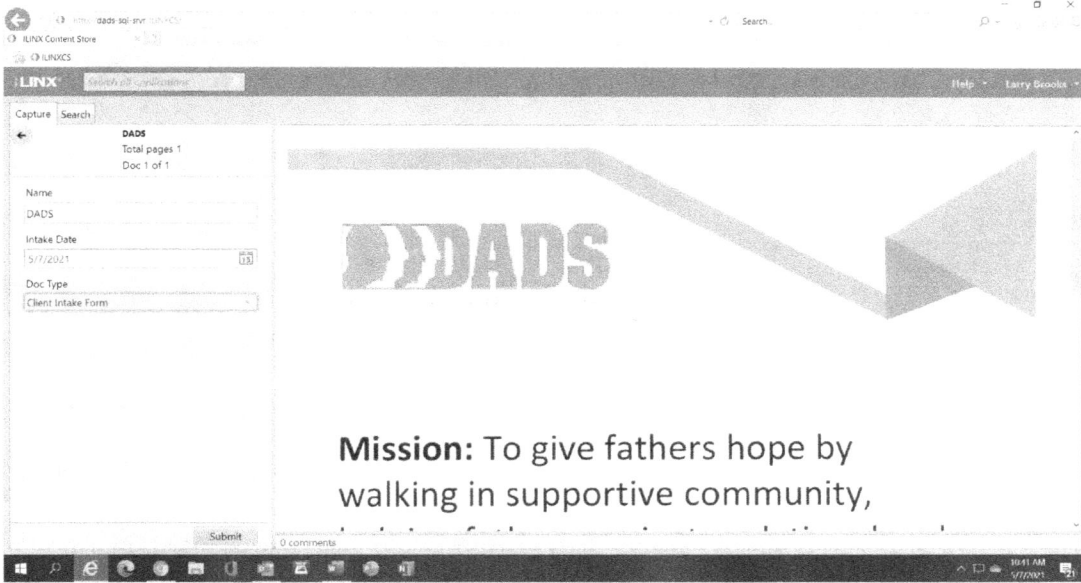

Click on **Submit**.

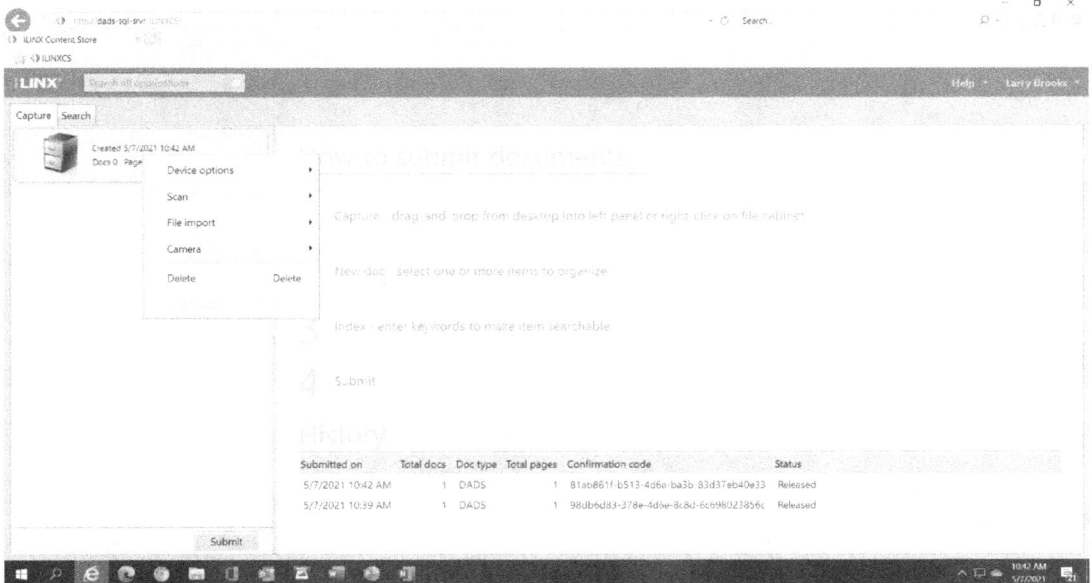

144　DOING DADS: INTAKE AND SUPPORT MANUAL

After you chick the Submit Tab, it will take you back to this screen. To make sure that you properly uploaded the documents click on **Search All Applications**.

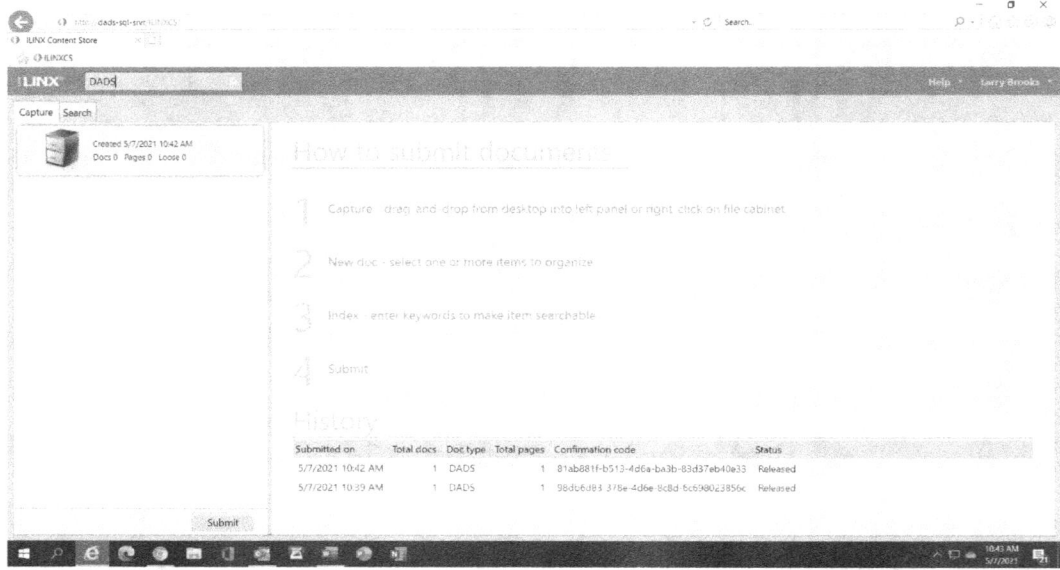

Type in client's name and hit Enter.

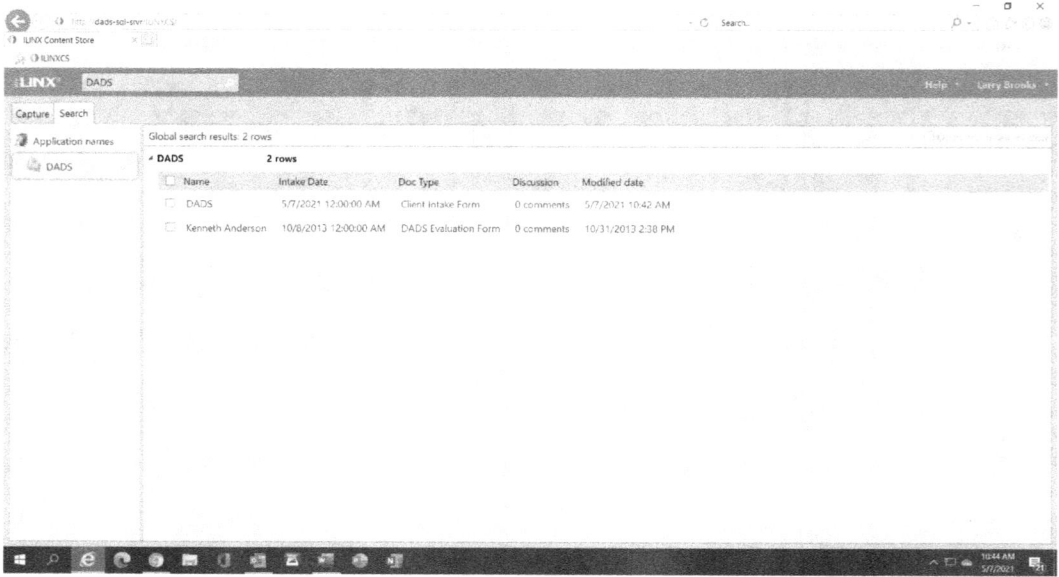

Congratulations you have successfully put the client's documents into **ILINKS.**

# CHAPTER FIVE

# 5.1 Ongoing Client Support

The National Fatherhood Initiative has identified fatherlessness as the root cause of $100 billion a year in taxpayer costs. That's why, at D.A.D.S., our primary focus is on reuniting men with their biological children and working with them to become responsible fathers. Over the last 21 plus years, DADS has helped 4,728 men reunite with over 12,573 children.

Through the D.A.D.S. process, these fathers are able to find and keep jobs, pay child support, purchase homes, and lead their families in ways that result in their children staying in school, off drugs, out of gangs and going to college. Our statistics speak for themselves:

1. Since 1998, D.A.D.S. has provided weekly support group services to more than 4700 men and over 12,500 children in Seattle and Tacoma, Washington. These groups give men critical coping and survival skills to relieve the stresses that place their families in danger of disintegration.
2. From 2001 to 2014 alone, fathers in Washington State who are D.A.D.S. clients increased monthly child-support payments by 12%, according to the state's Division of Child Support (DCS).
3. In that same time frame (2001 to 2014), fathers in Washington who were D.A.D.S. clients reduced the total amount of back child-support payments to their children by an additional $10.8 million, according to the DCS. This number has only continued to climb.

## Practical Ways to Help

The effectiveness of the D.A.D.S. program depends on the trust that each individual develops in our staff, our process, and the community. D.A.D.S. does not charge for our services. We invest in building a vision for healthy fatherhood in several different ways:

- **Navigating the system (as outlined in this manual)**: D.A.D.S. helps men understand the process, forms, and documentation to successfully navigate the legal system related to child support, back payments, parenting plans, and visitation.
- **Addiction services:** D.A.D.S. helps men find the support necessary to live lives that are drug and alcohol free.
- **Client support:** D.A.D.S. offers a weekly Bible study and other relational support and accountability opportunities.

The following story, told in Marvin Charles' book, *Becoming Dads: The Mission to Restore Absent Fathers* (available on Amazon.com), illustrates what this component of the D.A.D.S program can look like.

Mac was a 26-year-old father of two children who connected with us following some jail time (charged with a felony), and working a few menial jobs after he got out of prison. When Mac came to us for help connecting with his children, we challenged him to take some serious steps. Our D.A.D.S. team helped him get a car and provided a place for him to live until he got a job and got on his feet, which he did. We encouraged him to begin sending money to the mother of his children. This was his chance to create his own environment, take responsibility, and be empowered to make changes. Unless he did this, we counseled him, he would never be able to become involved in his children's life.

We told Mac, as we tell all the men who come to us, "Give yourself two years to create something, to get some work history, to get on a program where your kids can be on your medical insurance if possible. This is the foundation you need, something you can build on."

We also told him, "You've got to put yourself to the side and let go of 'you,' and start doing 'them.'" This is common message our clients need to hear, over and over again.

Very often, a typical D.A.D.S. client is living a lifestyle that answers to nobody else but himself. He is not grasping (at first) what it is going to take for him to become involved in his children's lives in a healthy, positive way. Most of these men have never really considered (or even seen modeled) what it looks like to be in a caring, reciprocal relationship where they give sacrificially for another person's well-being. Many, if not most of them, have grown up with an attitude of survival and self-interest, and this translates into their most personal relationships.

It takes time, relational investment, training, and life-to-life role modeling—"walking alongside"—to help them learn these life lessons, and that's what the Ongoing Client Support aspect of D.A.D.S. aims to provide.

## 5.2 Support Meetings

The real ministry of D.A.D.S. is not what we do in our services for men but in the ways that God transforms people. We live in such an information culture; mere words have lost their impact. What really impacts hearts is when faith and hope put on feet and hands.

For example, Bob was a young man in his early forties who spent 16 years in prison, entering the correctional system for selling drugs. He had two children in another state. Following his release, he desperately wanted to live a normal life and re-connect with his children.

Besides the logistical help of navigating "the system," Bob needed a support system around him who could walk alongside him, as well as connections who could offer him, or help lead him to, a work opportunity.

Over the years, we have accumulated just such a support group in our donors and volunteers who actively support and engage in the work of D.A.D.S.. These people understand the depth of the battle these men face, but also the healing power of Jesus at work through ordinary people. They trust the combination of practical steps we help men take in working through the system, and the power of support that comes from opportunities like the weekly Bible study we hold in our D.A.D.S. office.

What happens in our Wednesday morning Bible study at our office is amazing. Men from different backgrounds, races, and economic backgrounds gather around the common pursuit of life, faith, and fatherhood, and something extraordinary happens. They begin to care about each other and start to go to bat for one another, practically living out what it means to live in an accountable community as men who are imperfect but love one another. This breaks the attitude that American men have adopted from both ends of the socio-economic spectrum, "Just look out for Number One because nobody else will look out for my good but me."

As we walk someone like Bob through his paperwork, or give a man like Mac some counsel in relating to his child's mother, we invite him to walk with the other men who are going through the same process, or have walked through it and are on the other side. The power of D.A.D.S. is for these men to see other men's lives transform, often in their attitudes first and then in their situations. They are not being told to change, but they are watching other men change and learning how to walk the same path. Success stories beget more success stories.

It is not only what men like Bob see when they go to the groups, but also what they are able to process and express themselves through their journey—that they are not alone. That keeps them encouraged to persevere on a healthy course. They see how a walk of faith and intentional fatherhood is lived out, however imperfectly, by men like themselves.

# 5.3 Fatherhood Training

More than anything else, it is developing positive relationships with their children that encourages and motivates men to lead more constructive lives. However, most of the men we see have no idea how to BE a father.

For one thing, most of them have had very little contact, or at least irregular contact, with their children up to this point. According to a Pew Reach Center report, about half of fathers who don't live with their kids only see their children a few times a year, or have no visits at all. In addition, almost one-third of those fathers correspond with their kids over the phone or via email less than once a month.* Roughly one in five fathers who live apart from their children say they visit with them more than once a week, and an additional 29% see their children at least once a month. For 21% of these fathers, the visits take place several times a year. And for 27%, there are no visits at all.

So, can you imagine, when the fathers do get custody of their children, or begin participating regularly in parenting activities, how ill-equipped they can feel? This is another area where a supportive community can step in and provide training, encouragement, and resources.

## The Becoming D.A.D.S. Course Curriculum

The men we see at D.A.D.S. generally find themselves in a different situation from the average person in the general population who simply wants to improve his parenting skills, who already has at least a foundational understanding of what it means to be a dad. Most of the men we see—who have come through the prison system, who have spent their lives in dysfunctional family settings, on the streets, or who have never had an involved dad

---

\* Gretchen Livingston and Kim Parker, "A Tale of Two Fathers," Social and Demographic Trends: Pew Research Center: June 15, 2011. http://www.pewsocialtrends.org/2011/06/15/a-tale-of-two-fathers/#living-apart-from-the-kids. Accessed 27 September, 2015.

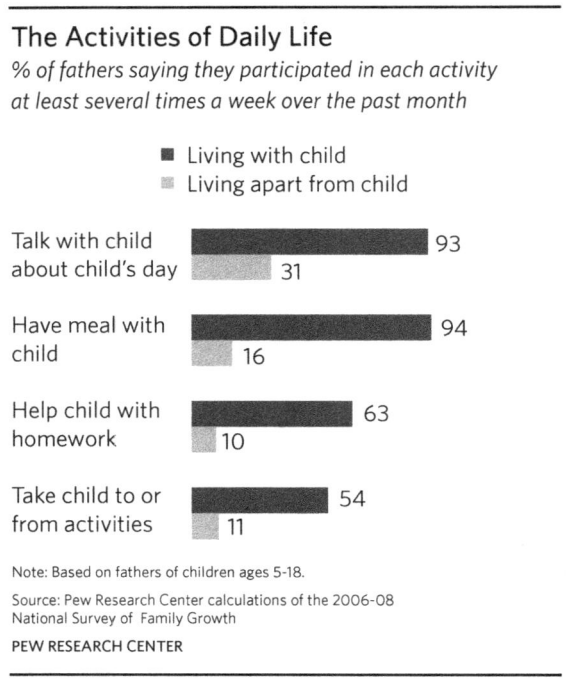

themselves (many of our D.A.D.S. dads relate to all these categories simultaneously)—have no idea what it looks like to be a good father.

Following are a few of the most common and important parenting principles we emphasize with the men in our D.A.D.S. program. These are key to helping them overcome the patterns of their past and build healthy new ones for the future. These principles include:

1. **Learning to appropriately express both negative and positive emotions**, and to meet their children's emotional needs. Men in general, in our society, have been taught that it is appropriate to display certain emotions and supress others. However, many men, particularly those from disadvantaged or abusive upbringings, have suppressed and denied healthy emotions for so long that they no longer recognize them, nor are they able to handle them in the lives of others around them, such as their women and children. This puts them—and their children—at an extreme disadvantage in life. Through training and practice, and often some healing, they can learn to become emotionally healthy and create an emotionally healthy environment for their children.

2. **Communicating to connect with their children** through speaking and active listening. Many of the men we work with are not parenting full time and need to learn to maximize the time they do have with their children. Relationships need to be cultivated and nurtured, and we do that through communication, which includes the words we say, the tone we use, the body language we reflect, and the listening we do.
3. **Learning to engage with their children** and entering their world through play and personal involvement. Being an involved dad means being intentional. It's not completely true that quality time beats quantity time. There needs to enough quantity to get good quality. Fathers have the unique privilege of introducing their children to the world and providing the safety and confidence for them to explore it. But if dads are uncomfortable with relating to their kids on the kids' level, this is made difficult. We help dads learn to play with their children at different levels, using things like songs, stories, make believe, and simple games. As the children get older, this would include more complex games and activities, sports, hobbies, camping, fishing, road trips, and cooking or baking together.

A key way we provide this training is though our fatherhood course: *Becoming D.A.D.S: An Innovative Fatherhood Curriculum.* The course is designed to educate and empower men in challenging situations to take the needed responsibility and action so their children can thrive and be successful for the next generation.

Once your D.A.D.S. program is up and running, this is another component you can add to serve the men who come through your doors. Participants in the *Becoming Dads* course will build knowledge, grow in self-awareness, and apply skills related to becoming the dads their children need. At the completion of this course, participants will be able to:

1. Face the truth of their past and have hope for a better future
2. Understand the impact of their role as a father
3. Know what their children need from them
4. Be committed to their children for a lifetime
5. Understand the character of a man who lives for others
6. Know how to have a healthy relationship with their children's mother(s)
7. Start on the road to healing and getting past hurdles to effective fathering
8. Have grounding in their spiritual walk and growth
9. Improve their employment situation
10. Understand the child support system
11. Get on track to providing child support to their children

This course comes with both participant and facilitator guides (available on Amazon.com or through the Washington D.A.D.S. offices. Please inquire for bulk discounts.

D.A.D.S. Seattle Office
411 12th Ave, Suite 300
Seattle, WA 98122
(206) 722-3137

D.A.D.S. Tacoma Office
10402 Kline St. SW
Lakewood, WA 98499
(253) 231-3164

www.aboutdads.org

# Acknowledgments

I am thankful, first of all, for my husband Marvin, who has stayed the course and path of the vision and mission that God gave him in 1999. With his tireless, relentless, and unselfish human efforts, and his trust and faith in God, as a team we have seen our vision reach across state and county lines. Marvin, my lifelong partner, you have made this journey worthwhile. I am so glad we get to do life together.

I also want to thank our children, who sacrificed much of their youth to patiently allow their parents to serve home and community. It was through the firsthand adverse conditions our children experienced that our family embraced faith in God. He helped us to heal as a family unit, which gave the children insight that to this day has allowed them to embrace the vision and mission of D.A.D.S. Our painful journey to reunify our family is the reason for the passion we share to see that other families have a chance to grow and stay together.

There are many great people to whom Marvin and I owe an enormous debt of gratitude: staff and board members (past and present), government officials, clergymen, and countless community partners that have walked alongside us to help build strategic relationships and partnerships over the years.

We want to give a special acknowledgment and thanks to the Casey Family Programs for their encouragement and support that made this project possible. We will always remember the words of Jim Casey: "One measure of your success will be the degree to which you build up others who work with you. While building up others, you will build up yourself."

D.A.D.S.' teams have rendered constructive critique and suggestions that helped to shape this book. They were always eager to test the new ideas, new ways of thinking, and new practices that enabled the team of D.A.D.S. to create this manual.

Thank you, each and every one of you; you are all a part of the beautiful work of reunification and restoration that is happening through the work of D.A.D.S.

*Jeanett Charles*
*Co-Founder, COO, and Executive Vice President*
*Divine Alternatives for Dads Services*

# About the Authors

## Jeanett Charles

Jeanett has two decades of human services working firsthand with dads in the nonprofit profession as Co-Founder, COO, and Executive Vice President at the D.A.D.S. organization. Jeanett's primary focus has been on client intake and child support system navigation for D.A.D.S. clients, laying the foundation for the principles and procedures that would form the essential content of this book.

In the 20 plus years since D.A.D.S. was founded, Jeanett and Marvin and their staff have helped over 4,700 fathers be reconnected to their families. In this time, they have built strong relationships with leadership at Washington State's Division of Child Support and Department of Social and Health Services, which allows them to work cooperatively to help D.A.D.S. clients and advocate for policies that make a positive difference for the families they serve. Jeanett and Marvin are regularly invited to speak at local, state, and national fatherhood and family events. They have eight children and a growing number of grandchildren, and live in Seattle, Washington.

# About the Authors

## Marvin Charles

Marvin is the founder and executive director of Divine Alternatives for Dads Services. For over 20 years, he has been effectively helping men reclaim their positive role as the fathers their children need. Marvin's own powerful story of separation and reunification with his family, parents, and children, fueled his passion for ministry, gave him experience, and earned the trust of other men to be their mentor and advisor.

Marvin is also an emerging national leader in creating stronger fathers and healthier families. He travels across the U.S. to speak about empowering fathers, to learn from other national leaders, and to share his successes with other organizations planning to implement fatherhood programs.

Marvin is the author of *Becoming Dads: The Mission to Restore Absent Fathers*, which chronicles his life and the beginnings of DADS. He is an ordained minister and his extraordinary effectiveness comes from his ability to see through the pain and threats of those he counsels to the powerful change possible by embracing a living God and larger purpose.

*www.aboutdads.org*

www.ingramcontent.com/pod-product-compliance
Lightning Source LLC
Chambersburg PA
CBHW081745100526
44592CB00015B/2306